Confessions of My Selves

Olivia Orfield

PublishAmerica
Baltimore

ISBN: 1-4137-5504-6
PUBLISHED BY PUBLISHAMERICA, LLLP
www.publishamerica.com
Baltimore

Printed in the United States of America

In Memory of My Husband

ACKNOWLEDGMENTS

I wish to express my thanks to many persons. I shall leave you unnamed for fear of inadvertently failing to cite a deserving helper.

First, I deeply appreciate my husband's support in all areas of our shared lives. I'm also especially indebted to my sons and their wives, and to my former psychoanalyst for your contributions to my personal growth.

I'm grateful to my instructors at Rice University, and to members of the psychological profession with whom I shared contact, for all I've learned from you. I'm thankful also to those of the Union Institute and University who guided me to my doctorate degree in philosophical psychology.

Members of our longtime writing group, my psychotherapeutic clients, my extended family and my other friends, you've greatly enriched my years.

To all of you, I offer my unbounded gratitude.

— Olivia Orfield

INTRODUCTION

I'm a psychotherapist, and the field of my doctorate is philosophical psychology. Only the expositional fourth portion in *Confessions of My Selves* is primarily "psychological." My first three groupings, in this order, are "philosophical," "spiritual" and "meditational." The fifth is "marital." Formats in which I express myself vary from part to part.

The initial triad consists of dialogues. Speakers—"I Outward," "I Inward" and "I Centered"—represent sides of myself. I intend them to indicate the direction at that moment of my interest and focus.

As "I Outward" my concern is the nature of cosmic, world and human reality external to me. Often this voice also includes me as belonging to the whole I'm discussing.

"I Inward" expresses my thoughts, emotions, intuitions, sensations and any other internal experiences relevant to their subject.

"I Centered" embodies a position of neutrality between the other two standpoints. It frequently is aware of both and can embrace the two simultaneously, or either of them or neither. Matters extending to this middle position may prove impersonal and also lie outside of realms which I term "Outward" and "Inward." Of these three perspectives it's medial "I Centered" who usually invents and articulates explanations.

Described briefly, "I Outward" states; "I Inward" personalizes; and "I Centered" questions.

My intent is to present my thought as a continuous flow, rather than as a focus on discrete aspects of myself.

Materials vary throughout section five, "Confessions of My Marital Self." Within it I wish to respect the privacies of all persons directly and indirectly involved. Disguises extend to my husband and me. Accordingly I rename and combine all identities including our own. They meld with those of individuals I've known and worked with.

Among the "journalisms" the movement of their sequence is chronologically forward.

Throughout the opening four-fifths of the book I offer innumerable statements of my surmises, beliefs, opinions and convictions. At least as frequently I express my perceptions, feelings and sensings. Any of these admissions, including those in "Confessions Five," which I don't openly and promptly contradict I offer as honest representations of who I am. All of them matter to me so fully I never could subject them deliberately to distortion. For they constitute my core.

I invite you to join me on a journey without destination. Why should you care to? Because my words are wise? Unique? Fascinating? I'm too partial to them to appraise them realistically. So I shall ignore my standards of self-judgment. I do suggest my thoughts can offer a backboard against which you may choose to bounce your own ideas. Or my self-explorings might evoke new concepts of your own.

Stay with me and I'll at least provide you contact with the inwardness of but-yet-another human being different from yourself. As we proceed I, too, shall investigate and discover more fully who I am. I wish a bon voyage to us both.

CONTENTS

Philosophical Confessions   *11*
    Chapters 1–9

Spiritual Confessions   *45*
    Chapters 1–10

Meditational Confessions   *77*
    Chapters 1–6

Psychological Confessions   *95*
    Chapters 1–13

Marital Confessions   *143*
    Chapters 1–29

Afterword   *231*

I

CONFESSIONS OF MY PHILOSOPHICAL SELF

1. AN ENVISIONING

I Centered

No one, in my view, can speak with proven infallibility on behalf of
what is. I'm therefore aware that I express here only my own
convictions and experience.

I Outward

For creating this chapter and the next I utilize portions of my
earlier book, *Vortex: A Personal Quest into the Nature of What Is*,
published by prism press in 1981.

I Inward

Now in one instant a journey commences. Frightened, elated, I
resign to whatever shall follow, suck breath.

Totally primary thusness transforms into me; the full of my body
flows back into it. Then vortex—Void giving birth—emits my self it's
born from. Vast I spread, faster, until I'm the cosmos, becoming each
moment a sole vortex: consciousness.

I Outward

All's utter encompassment: consciousness avowing itself in its
fluid, changing multiplicity to be One.

I Inward

It surrounds me, presses me, buoys me, closes my eyelids, drains
itself from me. Emptied, I listen, watch, through my skin...

I Centered

...where I hear and see this:

I Outward

The single is the many. Both are manifold and indivisible. Nor do outside, inside occur, for either's the same as, the face of, and is, the other. They're solely a unity.

I Inward

Around me all's a moving, twisting flux of color and form, spin into Void, whirl from new vortex into back/front, dark/light. All just the inescapable One.

I Centered

It's meaningless to speak of what at last I "know"; the case is what I am:

I Outward

The oneness of raw cosmic consciousness in its multiplicity. There's no "I"...

I Centered

...just consciousness; "mine," "my mind," only because I can't be all of manyness.

I Inward

My hands and feet confess they're me neither more nor less than my chair or yard are. Finally I'm free of prison:...

I Centered

...not sensing myself to be the universe.

I Outward

I am, and it is I. An "I" who now testifies...

...All's experience of and by utter encompassment: consciousness I shout to be One. The cosmos I deem objective is its subjective awareness of itself.

The One, remaining so, becomes and is many, thus knowing itself by beingness that's life.

I Inward

I exude though my pores to register I'm presences and places my ears and eyes connect me to.

I Outward

My comprehension responds: No single, inner centralness exists of consciousness in whole. As space, it's infinite, encompassing me and all events. Its centerings aren't inwardness nor outwardness; they're manifestations only.

I Inward

Constantly I sustain their becoming me and whatever is, occurring every or anywhere I turn.

I Centered

Each of their endless number is bulls-eye of the universe. For I just now understand that centering is simply irreducibility without differing from it one iota.

I Outward

I see: No other exists for the cosmos to relate with outside itself, beyond. And its void of all entity to circle inward toward.

I Inward

Knowing washes me guiltless.

Like each of us, I'm alone. Throughout our lives we wander corridors of only our own minds.

I Centered

Indescribable and total is the loneliness of mind, creation, drenched as it is throughout its marrow and my own with oneness.

2. CLIMAXING

I Inward

Now I'm cosmic center fanning its radiation that all experience is.

I Outward

I'm aware of the borning of polarity: pull-apart becoming fusion of rear/fore, dark/light, sound/sight. Two faces, each the other's backing, daring me to question...

I Centered

..."what does a between-you, if there be one, secret?"

I Outward

I observe their answer: Instead of harboring a middle, each convolutes into the other.

All transforms into its other face without prior distance or cleavage from it. The universe everlastingly is involution into opposite, the reason, then, that nothing is: It's instead continually the process of a metamorphosis into the moment's what it isn't.

I Centered

Thus no being that isn't becoming does or can ever occur.

I Outward

For each front, to exist, must include its back, and as its own alternate.

I Centered

Since in space each pinpoint and planet is nucleus, none is. With centering and non-centering thus meaningless...

I Inward

...I need no longer chain to focus.

I Outward

Voidness transmuting into suchness is consciousness.

I Centered

Its encompassing me is a field without interruption that I as a whole become: the shimmer and hum of continuum.

I Outward

Consciousness is the continuum of centering's convolution, of particle's waving. It's voidness and suchness, "opposites," in union that manifests as electro-energy the tension of their colliding.

I Inward

This hiding, shining unthinkable at last I can see and feel I incessantly become. This is my hour to know. All.

I Outward

So I attest that consciousness as one immeasurable present envelops the whole of its facet, time.

I Centered

Continuum's flux is pulsating and airily void. As am I, the spontaneous, constant creating of myself. Every and each type of being is mere arising, unagented, uncontrolled. I never again can forget I'm every second newborn.

I Inward

And I writhe for the fixity of plateau. Let there be womb to curl in that, like me, is refugee from encompassment by mindness, womb whatever I stare at combines to transform into until womb becomes once more what I see it always was and is: consciousness that's one.

I Centered

Mindness is empty of form or substance.

I Inward

As me, it's whatever I hear, look at, think, feel, in multiple changing, flux. It's my body and merely the content of my each moment's awareness. Unimprisoned at last from fantasy edges I presume to be me...

I Centered

...I recognize who I am:

I Outward

...the universe I encounter. Its entering into my senses I don't reflect but become. My harboring a mind is concept only; mindness itself I am.

I, visualizer, differ no mite from what I gaze on.

I Inward

To image or see it as I do, except for my body no agent exists.

I Outward

All including me is nothing but oneness of consciousness. I don't otherwise exist. As if "I" weren't unreal I can merely manifest emptiness.

Whatever dichotomy I devise of subject/object, knower/known, is to create or corner and capture a cogitator-I who isn't.

I Inward

This moment vestigial belief in my self dissipates; my survivings tumble throughout engulfment, frightened but free and everlasting.

No my mindness am I, no me. My eyes can no longer hallucinate the world I would carve apart and explain.

I Outward

Instead, they now see: All agency, entity, separation, is utter illusion.

I Inward

On either side of my lids all's underived, primary. Where avoid the insistence of thusness refusing the slightest withdrawal?

I Centered

I, without objectivity to echo, am subjectiveness particular, unique, unrepeatable each moment, total. I'm the perceiving itself of creating.

I'm excruciating certainty of oneness, agony and ecstasy of understanding. They're sole unbearable into a death that's compassion: suffering's forgiving itself. For not existing I commiserate with time, space, difference, and with my then's outside for its reversal into my now's inside, to overcome for me the whole of seeming.

I Inward

I fear to look anywhere, for everywhere what stares at me is the inside of my mind. Humanness that's I, or used to be, shudders with sobs at the finish of its dissipation: as illusion, as moon's dark side of this moment white with inferno's sun.

Heaven is hell. Agony is ecstasy.

I Centered

Swirling with cycles of birth and death , at last I writhe no longer from the pain and joy of bearing all of it. They flow into and mingle with serenity that's filled with the gratitude of comprehending myself:

I Outward

...River of life.

3. A VIEW OF DOUBTING

I Inward

I'm a would-be philosopher who no longer believes in concepts—their intrinsic or "objective" verity or meaning, nor their helpfulness. My beliefs pertaining to void/thus, continuum, consciousness, oneness, etc. appear to me today as my own theories, nothing more.

I Centered

Whether or not such concepts are accurate, "true," isn't judgeable.

I Inward

So I write this book to reconfirm for myself...

I Outward

...I've nothing to say of any inherent validity.

I Inward

In this way I hope to end my wearisome quest to know any kind of ultimate reality.

I Outward

My agnosticism tells me that basic what-is can't be discovered with the mind.

I Inward

Yet I don't consider I'm a nihilist.

I Outward

One of Webster's definitions of nihilism is this: "The belief that all existence is senseless and that there is no possibility of an objective basis for truth."

I Centered

Sense does occur, even if only as a concept in the minds of those postulating that all existence is meaningless. To me...

I Outward

...dichotomies such as sense and senselessness are false fabrications.

I Centered

In addition, I can't state with any assurance that "there 's no possibility of an objective basis for truth."

I Outward

I surely don't think a case for "objectivity" is makeable. But...

I Centered

...how could I, or anyone, know positively what the actuality is? Am I saying agnosticism is the only valid stance to take?

I Inward

For me, yes, which is just another opinion. In different words, the content of beliefs frankly no longer interests or intrigues me...

I Centered

...as representing per se validity.

I Inward

Not so, the process of believing, a function like digestion, bladder and anal elimination, feeling, etc.—any part of human activity.

I Outward

To what extent do constructs of mine happen to coincide with actuality?

I Centered

I can't decide with certainty.

I Outward

No one in my view can certify the correctness of any viewpoint.

I Centered

The content of thought doesn't reflect or mirror its subject matter, but, rather, is product of the human process of thinking.

I Inward

Ideas of mine merely manifest portions of me. By accepting that at least in my mind this situation is the, or a, reflection of factual reality, I hope I harm no one, myself included.

I Centered

I don't know that any statements I make are true, nor do I know they're false. They testify to merely my present, personal vision. What's so—actual—and what isn't I've no idea. I'm agnostic about all ideation.

I Outward

Atheism declares: "Concepts don't express truths." Agnosticism postulates: "Concepts don't necessarily—repeat, necessarily— express truths."

I Centered

Although no proof exists, in my opinion, that any belief is true, no proof exists that it isn't, either.

I Outward

The label, "fact," is an appraisal and consequently is subjective. All such judgments and therefore all facts are internalizations. Existences other than persons aren't subjective (unless to themselves); they're actualities. As human experience, however, they become personal and conditioning subjectivities.

I Centered

All is projection—usually by humans—of occurrences within themselves.

I Inward

"I don't and can't know" spares worry...

I Centered

...about whether beliefs are true or false.

I Inward

If certainty is illusion...

I Centered

...belief isn't primary...

I Inward

...experience is.

I Outward

It's what-is: manifestation.

I Inward

And part of our experience—a crucial portion of it— is our believing.

4. A VIEW OF TIME

I Outward

At least some Buddhists stipulate that the physical cosmos has been always apparent.

I Centered

If they're correct, to me process would seem to manifest as probably cyclical and therefore repetitive.

I Outward

If, however, the material universe originated within duration it requires a beginning.

I Centered

Has the cosmos, then, always consisted at least in part of physical phenomena?

I Inward

For myself, as yet I've found no answer to this question.

I Centered

In any event, evolutionary process seems to me a likelihood.

I don't suggest, however, that I'm postulating all occurrence necessarily constitutes progress...

I Inward

...a value judgment I don't sustain.

I Outward

Defined a composite of past, present and future, time merely is useful concept.

I agree with the many persons who proclaim: In actuality whatever-is can occur always only within the eternal present.

And the now is preformed, if at all, in solely the single instant preceding it out of which it unfolds.

5. A VIEW OF ONENESS

I Centered

How are emptiness and oneness related, if at all?

I Outward

Neither is any kind of substance. Both are characteristics of the All.

I Centered

Because the cosmos is empty, it is one? Does voidness underlie the generativity of consciousness and its culmination in awareness?

I Inward

To me it all would seem so, yes.

I Centered

Perhaps oneness provides the "glue" of the non-fragmentation, indivisibility, inherent in All.

I Outward

Oneness isn't really a quality of voidness but a result, an aspect, of it.

Void is "sunyata," or, roughly, the Buddhist's emptiness; consciousness and its myriad manifestations of what-is coincide with "tathata" ("suchness").

Oneness is of course omnipresent...

I Centered

...and merely another term for the boundlessness of emptiness.

I Inward

This thought occurs to me: A main reason that sensing oneness, or becoming it, yields ecstasy isn't merely because it's an apprehension of basic fact, or that it's a homecoming into what-is for the individual consciousness. No, in humans the effect of oneness occurs from its reflection of the fundamental rapture contained in and expressive of existence itself.

I Outward

A second idea: Per se bad could occur in only a righteous cosmos cleaved. And not if all agency, entity, separation is, as I believe, utter illusion.

I Centered

The universe, its no one beat of its vibrate , is the dance ecstasy of absolute and total yes.

I Inward

This moment I can feel the simultaneity, the unity, of manyness and oneness.

I Centered

Although to me all consciousness is in union, I'm not convinced that oneness in its totality necessarily is consciousness. How do I wish to define consciousness? I don't...

I Inward

...but if to satisfy a part of me I must...

I Centered

...I'll term it energy.

6. A VIEW OF CONSCIOUSNESS

I Centered

I'll review for my clarification my ideas of cosmic foundation, with which I still agree.

I Outward

All's one eternal consciousness that's void: fluid, changing, non-obstructing, permeable.

Voidness transmuting into suchness, thusness, is consciousness.

This consciousness is the continuum of centering's convolution, of, in science-phrase, particle's waving. It's voidness and suchness, "opposites," in union that manifests as electro-energy the tension of their colliding.

No single inner centralness exists of consciousness in whole.

To proceed:

Characteristics, capacities, of consciousness are...

I Centered

...what?

I Outward

Awareness, potentiality and generativity, each interlocking with the other two and inseparable from them. Potentiality and generativity activate all energy/matter and coincide with it. Its behavior is process which, because occurring within time, requires a beginning.

I Centered

Consciousness is to me devoid of intent not manifest in matter.

As potential only, consciousness is, in my thinking, totally undifferentiated. Employing usual terminology, I consider it the cosmic "ground of being," with self-awareness its primary aspect.

I Outward

Potentiality inherent in the generativity of consciousness allows manifestation to occur. Immanent throughout whatever is, consciousness nonetheless preceded materiality in time and as its cause. Consciousness isn't limited to its appearance in and as phenomena.

I Centered

Another of the facets constituting consciousness, I'm thinking, is omnipresence. Consequently, I'll characterize constituents of consciousness as awareness of self and cosmos, and as potentiality, generativity and omnipresence. Awareness and potentiality seem to me not time-bound, unlike generativity and omnipresence which are.

I Outward

Evolution, in my view, is born of potentiality and generativity to become the process which is change.

I Centered

I now shall attempt to supplement my skeletal concepts I endorse above. Consciousness...

I Outward

...totally infuses primal energy.

Consciousness gives energy, in definition of both, its quality of vibrancy, electricality. Eruption of energy immediately activates awareness.

I Centered

In what fashion is consciousness present in all phenomena?

I Inward

To me, as forms of awareness evident throughout the universe.

I Centered

Do I stipulate that all consciousness is awareness?

I Inward

I believe I do.

I Outward

I'm certainly willing to commit to the premise that all awareness is consciousness.

I Inward

I'm dealing here entirely with concepts. I'm aware that these cogitations are, obviously, my personal representations. What do I actually and actively live? Oneness, voidness, awareness, the energy I am.

I Centered

Does void manifest only consciousness in various guises? Perhaps emptiness is source and its primary objectification is consciousness. My suspicion is that overt assertings of consciousness eventually are reabsorbed into the full of emptiness.

Do I postulate that all of is-ness , too, is consciousness? I'm thinking so.

I Outward

Below, above, beneath and beyond the All of thusness (manifestation, phenomena) is emptiness.

I Centered

So I'm really saying that within sunyata, the All, is manifestation and consciousness (awarenesses).

Is my present perspective, then, this: "Void manifests as consciousness?"

I Inward

This stance is rather a turnaround from my much earlier position that "All is one eternal consciousness that's void." I've certainly switched from citing "void" in adjectival form and made a noun of it. (And "consciousness," too, retains or regains noun status.) In other words...

I Centered

...I've given to void a more primal, more basic position within my theorizing (which is what this writing is) than I formerly assigned to it.

Am I ready to adopt the viewpoint that emptiness manifests only as consciousness? What if emptiness activates more extensively than as mere consciousness?

And would denying this possibility require my maintaining that all phenomena are forms of consciousness...

I Inward

...to wit, of awareness?

I Outward

A stand I can't force myself to take.

I Centered

Again, premises. I personally appear unable to avoid them. I excuse myself by remembering these words of, as I recall, Socrates: "The unexamined life is not worth living."

I Outward

Also, in my view: "The unexamined cosmos is not worth living in."

I Centered

Do I view consciousness as a facet or manifestation of emptiness?

I Outward

It's both.

I Centered

Does emptiness envelop consciousness?

I Outward

Yes, as it does all else. Emptiness to me evidences consciousness.

I Centered

Is consciousness the capacity of emptiness to manifest, phenomenalize?

In the present, at least, the idea of universal consciousness carries with it for me connotations of substance I reject.

I Outward

Sunyata (voidness), on the other hand, implies nothing of the sort.

I Inward

I now quite regularly feel all, my self included, to be empty. It's a transcendent and joyous experience I want not to lose.

I Centered

Are emptiness and consciousness synonymous terms? I don't think so. Concepts of consciousness clutter my version of voidness. If I'm bent on conceptualizing...

I Inward

...which obviously I am at present...

I Centered

...I want to simplify my premises as much as possible. Is consciousness present in all materialization?

I Outward

Yes, but only as forms of awareness evident throughout the universe.

I Inward

Whenever I've tried to sense or connect with consciousness in my "outer" world, or even my "inner," I've struggled. I've projected, I realize, my ideas of consciousness into the scene I'm viewing, and consequently muddied it. Clarity was rare and lasted a very brief while, such as a few seconds. Finally, when I look at or listen to "the thing in itself" I've no difficulty with connecting and staying in touch with it.

I feel a bit unhappy about the prospect of "abandoning" consciousness. I'd the same guilt sensation over "betraying" oneness in my worrying about consciousness: a concept very dear to me...

I Outward

...as is, I admit, emptiness.

I Centered

I confess, too, that my concepts of consciousness do seem to clutter...

I Inward

...what? My vision of voidness?

I Outward

Yes.

I Inward

It, too, excites me.

I Outward

From this minute on it's to emptiness alone that I assign its single power: to manifest.

I Centered

My present task is to reconsider "ground of being." Is it for me still "consciousness?" Or shall I now vote for "emptiness?"

7. A VIEW OF EMPTINESS

I Centered

How shall I describe emptiness?

I Outward

Of and out of emptiness whatever-is arises. All's born in, of, and all is, voidness, which is utter plenitude in unobstructing union, nonmanifest/manifest/nonmanifest.

Emptiness: that which is the unknowable, unspeakable, ultimate mystery...

I Centered

...the ungraspable, immaterial inscrutability, as itself hidden and unapparent.

I Outward

It also is the source, energy, spirit of all that is.

I Centered

It can be experienced only through sensing and participating in the oneness and transparent presence of the entire cosmos, through awareness of all that in any way is evident and accessible in the moment, and through openness to one's own uprisings and totality of responsiveness.

I Inward

I feel—not think—that in its indivisibility emptiness is the Buddhist "sunyata" or voidness: indefinable, incomprehensible...

I Centered

...ineffable, it then is of necessity fluid, nonobstructing, permeable. Is it "ground of being," "God," apparent in manifestation?

I Outward

It evinces whatever is, including consciousness, particular or universal, in any or all of its guises.

I Inward

But am I describing merely my personal concepts? Solely, at least, no, if voidness is "ground of being" itself and not merely an arising from it.

I Centered

The phrase "ground of being" for me connotes negatively. "Ground" seems primarily foundational as contrasted with inclusive. I prefer "field of being" as a description of the All. As for oneness...

I Outward

...it isn't really a quality of voidness but its result. Of course omnipresent, oneness is but another term for the boundlessness of emptiness.

All including the phenomena of consciousness returns into the Buddhist "sunyata." Nothing contains absolute, fixed edges or parameters. For whatever-is changes.

Because of emptiness, no boundaries are actual...

I Centered

...that is, they're not tangible. If every perimeter is illusory and all is unitary, no division that's real exists between objective "out there" and subjective "in here." "Inside," "outside" in actuality don't exist. They're one.

And manifestations of voidness?

I Outward

Unlimited in their oneness with allness but otherwise "edged" as particularities.

I'm finally willing to postulate that consciousness is a manifestation, not an integral facet, of the voidness which envelops it.

I Centered

The idea of universal mindness newly carries with it for me connotations of substance. These I find erroneous and not implied in the least by "sunyata." They now clutter my inner version of emptiness. I bid them farewell.

I'll support my earlier suspicion that consciousness episodically becomes apparency and then is reabsorbed into voidness.

As nonmanifestation consciousness is...

I Outward

...yes, emptiness.

This voidness, in its birthing and parenting of all possibility, creates fullness, tangibility, phenomena.

I Inward

My own case is not that I sense my oneness with all else. Rather, it seems to me as if the unity of all as active agenting infuses my experience and includes me. I feel myself to be the recipient of cosmic indivisibility.

I Outward

Emptiness and "field of being," since each is infinite, must coincide. With both lacking boundaries, they can't distinctly and discretely compartmentalize from one another. They're synonymous terms.

I Centered

Our knowledge of "ultimate basic reality" is always subjective and partial. Yet the object of any search for it is unlimited. At best, our apprehension and/or experience of all that's infinite, even if coincidental with its actuality, envelops only a portion of its total.

I Outward

Whatever absolute we seek is boundless, the reason it's unknowable.

I Centered

This voidness isn't, however, unlivable, unreachable. A Christian might claim we know it in, through and as the Holy Spirit aspect of God.

"Look within you" for "the truth" and for knowledge and experience of God, many say.

I Inward

And within us is the bulls-eye area for experiencing emptiness: we ourselves.

I Outward

Voidness manifest is thusness, suchness. It's affirmation, love.

In nature this emptiness is nonmanifest in any mode except as phenomena.

I Centered

Can it be that voidness concentrated is a black hole? Is the reverse side of voidness, paradoxically, utter and total compression? If absolute potential is concretized, could the result prove to be a seeming nothingness which actually is a containment of the All? Does it magnetize all available manifestation, then transform it into an electric allness/oneness which becomes a big bang?

I Inward
The questions invading my mind are these:
I Centered
If emptiness is boundless, doesn't it permeate all phenomena? In what manner?

8. A VIEW OF MANIFESTATION

I Centered

I feel the cosmos manifests as process: perpetual becoming that's empty of every shred of existence, reality, but one...

I Outward

...coreless rhythm of all moving. Nowhere is any essence. Unforeseen, unplanned, unpurposeful, all's here and now, nonexisting as other than myriad manifestation...

I Inward

...airy and fluid in its pulsation.

I Outward

Each thing and body exists through assuming forms in endless, utter change...

I Inward

...of flowing into one another.

I Centered

All is-ness—sight, sound, thought, feeling, judgment—is simply a circumstance of the universe. It contains no other intrinsic merit or meaning.

I Outward

Every phenomenon including experience is absolute in itself. The single reality of the universe is that which is.

Whatever basicness exists is apparent in, manifested by, objects and actions themselves. Each is a different form of any "field—or ground—of being" extant, and not in any fashion separate from it.

I Centered

"Objective criteria" are nonexistent as actuality apart from any agenting of experience. Where and how would such criteria occur? As a clump of energy in space? An impossibility, in my view.

I Outward
In other words, objective criteria can't exist as stable, fixed entities. For all is without boundary. All is flow. All alters, is change.

I Inward
No manifestation occurs external to me that observes, judges the phenomena I am.

I Centered
The reason? Because without barriers, which I believe don't exist, to serve as realities, any such watchfulness would fuse with the object of its attention. The two would become one. Manifestation doesn't occur as a self-contained entity unto itself—not in my view...

I Outward
...because it's devoid of essence of its own. It consists of and requires objects, bodies, happenings, in order to bespeak itself.

I Centered
Manifestation, to express my point differently, isn't a solitary essence.

I Outward
Why isn't it? Because it's empty. For the exercise of its powers it creates and utilizes agents through which it activates (manifests, phenomenalizes). It doesn't operate independently of all foci. Manifestation isn't self-containable, aloof from the specifics which it creates.

I Centered
I've always hypothesized that infinite potential is devoid of all apparent characteristic. So are black holes, except for their capacities to magnetize to the point of devouring their surroundings. I'm intrigued that the rims of black holes emit energy in the form of streams, or bands, of light.

I Outward
It has seemed to me that creation is a matter of rhythm: implosion and explosion.

I Centered
Is implosion the return to oneness and explosion the phenomenalizing of particularization? Does implosion's "overload" culminate in the explosion of a "big bang"?

I Outward
I've for some time entertained an intuitive suspicion that throughout time and space black holes and big bangs oscillate.

I Centered
Their rhythm perhaps creates and enacts the transmutation of one phase of manifestation into the other, its seeming opposite.

I Inward
Riddle: What's on the far side of a black hole? Suggested answer: A big bang.

I Centered
If the universe was and is eternally present in material form, what of potentiality? How would it fit into any concept of a cosmos not requiring creation?

Yet change, I concede, could occur.

I Outward
It's synonymous in the Buddhist view, as I understand it, with potentiality. Like the Buddhists, I consider possibility and actuality are separate only in a dichotomizing mind.

I personally can't embrace any postulation of the eternalness of manifest matter.

I Centered
What if both manifestation and change are illusions? I possess no proof that they aren't...

I Outward
...nor that they are.

I Inward
In either case I merely proceed with my life.

I Centered
The thought, somewhat relevant to the preceding remarks, also occurs to me that the universe is the product of a conflict between two opposing forces: "binding" and "separating."

I Outward
A variation of this idea comes to me: Each and every energy occurs in conjunction with its opposite, or other, side: for example, attraction and repulsion.

I wrote earlier that "all transmutes into its other face, into its 'what-it-isn't,'" or words to that effect. All transmutes, and therefore into some other visage, but not necessarily into its reverse; rather, it becomes a facet possibly just a bit different from its formerness on the spectrum of possibilities (meaning: potentialities of becoming actualities).

I Centered

Transmuting, at least in full, perhaps isn't necessarily a constant process. Opposites can exist, it seems to me today, merely in conjunction side-by-side with their shadow otherness.

In addition, can't large-scale transmutation manifest so slowly it appears not to be actual? And need it happen always as its complete opposite, rather than as a shift to a small degree? Whether each case is one of variation or total transformation depends, doesn't it, on definition?

Is any of what I've written "true?"

I Outward

If thoughts, emotions, intuitions, sensations and other similar manifestations were merely material, exclusively brain, they would evidence finite boundaries.

I Inward

All this cogitation is exactly that: theory, structure, and hard for someone like me to relinquish, caught up for a lifetime, as I've been, in this kind of mental gymnastic.

Following my moment's urge, I shall continue it below.

I Outward

Every manifestation occurs against the limitation of what it is not. A god constrained in any way is flawed, thereby contradicting attributable perfection.

I Centered

How, then, can the deity manifest even as potentiality?

I Outward

I apparently am postulating a god who is powerless.

I Centered

Possibly I'm overlooking what?

I Outward

Nonmanifestation isn't pure vacantness. It's infused with the capacity to evidence happening. Were it not, the cosmos would consist only of "field, or ground, of being" minus all event.

I Centered

Am I defining God as "field of being?"

I Outward

But not thereby succeeding in describing the essence or whole of deity.

I Inward
Any picture I paint of divinity would represent only myself.
I Centered
Who knows—about any of my possible articles of faith?
I Outward
Emptiness is to me boundless.
All, furthermore, belongs to the totality of manifestation.
I Centered
And the source of all phenomena? Hidden, mysterious. Experience of it is always partial.
I Outward
Consequently it's never comprehensible in whole. The how of form's arising is a veiled secret no more amenable to discovery than is the whole of consciousness or voidness.
I Centered
We as selves can experience, know, only the evidence which greets us but not its origin.
I do maintain all is mysterious and unknowable. But that statement, too, is concept.
I Outward
All I can assert with near-certainty is this: Some form of manifestation is.
I Centered
"Phenomena" describes occurrences within or stemming from an "objective" perspective. Viewing the term as "subjectivity"...
I Inward
...I'll name it "experience," if I'm determined to categorize.
I Outward
All supposedly signifies something else. Importance lies presumably in the "truth" or "reality" symbolized. Yet the perceivable world constitutes basic reality as actuality, not signification. Everything is itself...
I Inward
...and I'd like to respond to it as its own being only. Otherwise, I dilute my reaction to it.
I Centered
When I forego my pressings and reachings for contact with ultimate reality I'm left with this intuition:

I Outward
All manifestation is empty. Its every event is trackless...
I Inward
...traceless.

I Centered
Yet I haven't so far fully connected voidness with whatever-is, have I?

9. A VIEW OF UNION

I Centered

I did and can state that the only premise of which I'm reasonably certain is this: Manifestation occurs—I think. But it connects how with emptiness?

I Outward

To consider that basic reality underlies the perceptual world yet is different from it is a false dichotomy.

I Centered

I do believe all phenomena are empty.

I Inward

Why do I? Because of my own experience with voidness (synonymous with emptiness).

I Centered

Is my contention concerning the emptiness of phenomena also logical? I can answer "yes" for this reason: All is change; emptiness is a requirement and necessity of change.

I Outward

Were all phenomena boundless and total, no particularization could evidence. Capacities of manifestation, if occurring at all under such circumstance, would prove impotent and useless.

Any cosmic intentionality is nonspecific. The limits of unboundedness are only those which define specific foci of manifestation.

Concerns involving the beneficence and/or malevolence of the deity are anthropomorphisms. People don't constitute the center of the universe's interest or purpose. I consider emptiness/manifestation to be essentially amoral, especially when viewed from a human standpoint.

I Centered

My sense of voidness is my experience of manifestation, what-is. I needn't laud one type of experience over another. Thusness doesn't require my affirmation, not even for merely my own sake. Whatever happens within me is indeed manifestation, is-ness. All judgments of its various merits are merely my own.

I Outward

Emptiness, incorporating its power of manifesting, is the mysterious, unthinkable, unknowable "field of being" which is "God."

I Inward

The deity can be known experientially in part, at least, as emptiness.

I Centered

So let me revise my basic belief I stated earlier:

I Outward

Manifestation is empty, void...

I Centered

...yet, I think, as paradox does occur.

I Outward

Change is, as with oneness, a result, not an aspect, of voidness.

To me the thought that energy-as-matter constantly evolves makes obvious sense.

I Centered

Does emptiness envelop consciousness?

I Outward

Yes, as it does all else.

Emptiness manifests consciousness omnipresent throughout all visages of the cosmos.

I Centered

How do I wish to state my stand?

I Outward

Manifestation and the awarenesses constituting consciousness are emptiness.

I Inward

Nowadays, at least, the idea of universal consciousness carries with it for me connotations of substance; "sunyata" implies nothing of the sort. I reject the premise of content as feasible.

I'm aware that "Here I go again with my conceptualizing"...

I Centered

If I'm bent on conjecturing, which obviously I am at present, I'll attempt to simplify future premisings as much as possible.

Is consciousness the capacity of emptiness to manifest, phenomenalize? I doubt it. Is consciousness present in all materialization? Yes, as forms of awareness to me evident throughout the universe.

I Inward

I'm weary of my search for demarcations. I'm deciding not to accuse myself of lacking insight if I drop consciousness from my own basic premise. I'm hardly obligated to experience personally all possibilities.

I Centered

I'm not prepared to state that all of void is coincidental with consciousness. All of consciousness is certainly void, but not all of void necessarily is consciousness. Yes? No? Perhaps?

I Outward

For me, consciousness doesn't manifest void. The case is vice versa: Void manifests consciousness.

Am I now ready to assert:"Void manifests entirely as consciousness?" Only if I maintain that all manifestation is a form of the awareness which is consciousness.

I may not care to declare that all consciousness is awareness, but I'm certainly willing to commit to the premise that all awareness is consciousness.

I Inward

In the past my difficulty may have been: I attempted to connect with consciousness and not with emptiness or with the is-ness of phenomena. For the manifestations of consciousness are varied, whereas voidness is uniform.

But at the moment I see no harm in reaching toward an experiencing of consciousness, or oneness, and certainly emptiness, if impulses occur spontaneously. My sense of voidness, though, has proved on the whole the most fruitful of my meditations. I do consider that openness to emptiness "jumps back" to it as the "arena" most basic of all. This "fact" perhaps explains why it has offered me greater success than has the pursuit of availability to oneness or consciousness.

I Outward

I wish to state:

Void is boundless manifestation, appearing, changing, disappearing, as other phenomena arise.

Emptiness can manifest only without fixed form, substance or boundary.

What, summarized, are my primary tenets connecting emptiness and manifestation?

Emptiness is unknowable.

Manifestation is emptiness.

Experience is manifestation.

To amplify my terminology:

All manifestation is self-experience.

Thought is experience only.

"Emptiness" I described earlier in the words that follow, as: voidness, the unknowable, unspeakable, ultimate mystery, the ungraspable, immaterial, inscrutable, hidden, and unapparent. It also is the source, energy, spirit, of all that is. Again, I contend:

I Inward

"It can be experienced only through sensing and participating in the oneness and transparent presence of the entire cosmos, through awareness of all that in any way is apparent and accessible in the moment, and through openness to one's own uprisings and totality of responsiveness."

I Outward

It's "ground, or field, of being," "God," whose "doing" portion is apparency, manifestation.

"Unknowable" is the unthinkable, inconceivable through concept or intellection, perceivable only intuitively, experientially, as both internal and external happening.

I Centered

"Manifestation" is apparency both material and immaterial, phenomena, specific occurrence in past and present time. It's "being" that incorporates "being"'s source; it's the comprehensible, often available to the senses, and the inner sensing of its presence. It's materiality both worldly and cosmic.

I Inward

"Experience" is totally and always one or more of the aspects of manifestation. When its agent or recipient is sentient it is sensory, occurring externally as sensation; when internal it's thought, emotion, intuition.

I Centered

Nonsentient hosts are the receivers of happening affecting them.

I Inward

"Self-experience" is the aware or unaware response of all existences, no matter whether they're sentient or nonsentient, to their present and impacting situations.

I Outward

"Thought" is intellectual effort and its results, theorizing, idea formation which can be serious or trivial, wispy or grounded and elaborate. It involves and requires conceptualizing, no matter how fleeting, and consequently to varying degrees must employ language.

I Centered

Why, I ask myself, does void manifest...

I Outward

...thusness? My brain flashes its reply: The question's answer to me is the mystery, inscrutability, unknowability, of the nature of beingness.

Void in itself is boundlessly self-manifesting. Were it not, a compartmentalism would occur between void and its capacity to objectify. I repeat: Emptiness (I use the word as a synonym for void) is actually the capacity to manifest, phenomenalize.

Void is change, but, as with oneness, its changing is a result, not an aspect, of voidness. For...

...in brief, void is boundless manifestation, appearing, changing, disappearing, as other phenomena arise. I now and at last think...

I Inward

...feel and affirm that...

I Outward

...Void and manifestation are indivisibly, seamlessly one.

To simplify, what now are my premises?

    Emptiness is manifestation.

    All consciousness is manifestation.

    Consciousness is awarenesses.

In a fundamental amplification, I add:

    All is the self-manifestation of emptiness (unboundedness).

Consciousness and experience are manifestation.

Experience is awarenesses.

I wish to repeat in emphasis this encapsulation of my entire and newly formulated philosophy: All is the self-manifestation of emptiness (unboundedness).

I Centered

Why the particular appearances that occur and not, instead, others? I view responses to existing stimuli as the instruments of diversification. They create a web of connectedness in which forms appear, fade and reappear.

I Inward

To be aware is half the requirement for tuning in to emptiness/manifestation.

The other half is to allow experience without attempting to direct it.

I Outward

Voidness manifests whatever-is, including consciousness, particular or universal, in any or all of its guises.

I Centered

Consciousness can make itself known, I believe, as a boundless universal. This premise isn't a claim to the bedrock status for it belonging only to voidness.

I Outward

To connect with statements below, once more I maintain:

All is the self-manifestation of emptiness (unboundedness).

And:

All manifestation is consciousness.

All consciousness is energy.

All energy is experience and awareness.

Does emptiness extend beyond manifestation? In my view, the answer is yes, and for this reason: Emptiness is autonomously and indigenously self-manifesting, but manifestation isn't autonomously and indigenously self-emptying. Voidness conceivably could occur without manifesting. Phenomena, on the other hand, require emptiness in order to transpire.

Voidness and manifestation are indivisible but, paradoxically, not identical.

Because of emptiness, no barriers exist. Because of boundless manifestation, consciousness occurs without containment, yet paradoxically retentive of its identity within voidness.

Beyond even its own self-manifestation, in an infinite realm of silence and stillness only Void, often named God, remains.

The miracle that underlies and surpasses all others is, as many persons have stated, the apparent fact that anything is at all...

I Centered

...for which I glorify this God I term Emptiness.

II

CONFESSIONS OF MY SPIRITUAL SELF

1. A MYTHOLOGIZING

I Inward
I meditate and visualizations arise.
Myth still lives in and as me, while for this hour I witness:
I Centered
My garden of Eden is oneness encompassing twos and manyness, unbearably paradise that my snakelike recoil persuades my forever freshly divided self not to experience.
I Outward
Thus I renounce my reunification, choosing instead to dichotomize, label and moralize. Thereby further splitting, almost finally but never quite...
I Inward
...I fall into blindness of not perceiving my unity with what appears to be merely multiplicity: All.
I Centered
As for the serpent...
I Inward
...in one instant I sense in my bones it preceded in existence all division into realms of good and evil.
I Outward
Restless to move beyond its own primordial and encapsulating oneness which it shied away from...
I Centered
...this potent creature embodied and enacted "the divine itch": a craving for the individuation which is selfness...

I Outward

...and its exploring of possibility. God's warning is of forfeiting the sense of wholeness...

I Centered

...born of unity with the deity...

I Outward

...hence the prohibition against eating the fruit of knowledge. It is the violation of this directive by Adam and Eve that consigns God to the role of "other."

I Centered

Tasting the fruit served as the birthpangs of their individuality.

I Outward

The right to selfness was fought for and attained in the act of disobeying God...

I Centered

...the struggle and price required of them for the attainment of personhood...

I Outward

...with the activation of human freedom and potential the prize...

I Inward

...which nonetheless must be fought for...

I Outward

...the prohibition, therefore, against eating the fruit of knowledge...

I Centered

...because without some other against which or whom one defines oneself, that self could not be born.

I Outward

God perhaps deliberately inaugurated personhood by formation of creatures who defied the divine will...

I Centered

...through exercise of their own choice. The fruit and the serpent are servants of God...

I Inward

. . .in the service of human self-discovery...

I Centered

...as it reaches for activation of potentialities which self-development offers.

I Inward

For me the impetus of the spiritual journey centers on rediscovery of "the All" to which the hunger points: a reuniting of individuation and oneness.

I Centered

Are "the Fall" and "Sin" synonymous?

I Outward

They differ, I think, in that "the Sin" precedes "the Fall from Grace" and causes it. "The Sin" is the splitting of self from original oneness: the making of two from one.

I Outward

"Original sin," then, is this: eating the fruit of self-consciousness.

And the covering themselves by Adam and Eve with fig leaves? Their acknowledgment of individuality.

I Inward

Perhaps the deity (of the Old Testament, one not lacking in emotion) felt at least a bit proud of his creatures for their spirit of adventure and courage of rebellion.

Woman, I can't resist noting, led the way into personhood.

2. A SYMBOLIZING

I Inward

Shut-eyed, I witness melding of multipresent circle and cross:

I Outward

Circle is convolution; its disk and centering, return and season. It's enclosure: vortex, spiral, funnel, womb. As circle moving is endless.

Cross is continuum. It stretches north, south, west, east, up, down, left, right to infinity and back. Both expanding and converging, it's simultaneity; duality only as misexperience.

As cross, polarities radiate to everywhere extention of their fusion: central joining of trunk with head, arms and legs, of core with extremities, where circle squares in a complementariness of both shapes. Mind's physicalness energized is cross.

I Centered

Religion is psychology externalized. For depicting crucifixion, cross as body with arms outstretched, giving, receiving, impaled, is necessity.

Jesus is consciousness fragmentized as man's experience...

I Outward

...recycling into singleness through Christ's dying and resurrection.

I Centered

And crucifixion is two poles of reverse directions. To the One it's becoming the many; to the many it's becoming the One. In each instance a process that's single:...

I Outward

...death of whatever is by its metamorphosis into its covert, other face, opposite it seemingly wasn't.

I Inward

Thus is my crucifixion, anyone's, Christ's, becoming and being not separatings but oneness. Because ecstatic it's masochism's experiential base.

But crucifixion is the same as resurrection...

48

I Outward

...and no resurrection without death; yet no death because no differences.

I Inward

Hence, help me, no escapes from consciousness: all-encompassment knowing its oneness, cognition that's the agony of crucifixion.

I Centered

All's absolute one. Christ is—now. And not at all. Jesus!

I Outward

The universe therefore I is very although imagined mind of God invented. For singly consciousness is.

3. MY THOUGHTS ON NONBELIEF

I Inward

I'm reaching for possible parallels between Christian theology and my own beliefs.

What are my reasons, I ask myself, for attempting to synchronize my concepts with those of Christianity?

I Centered

I'm in part searching for a community with which I feel at least some affinity.

I Inward

My deeper motivation is that I'm experiencing indefinable spiritual longing.

I Centered

I'm drawn to entering a church atmosphere, but with preconceptions of why I'm there as few as possible. My goal is to leave outcome open. Rather than faith I hope only for whatever experience the worship environment yields to me.

I Inward

Faith for me would constitute rolling loaded dice. Faith why? In what? How could I pray without, to some degree, predetermining answers?

I don't wish to pray. I don't want faith, not in anything.

I Centered

Either praying or believing, for me, would threaten to close off my receptivity to occurrence.

I Inward

To pray would turn God for me into an exterior object.

I Centered

I'm not eager for religious conviction of any kind. For current me it would smack of the conceptualizing I'm striving to leave behind me.

I Inward

I hope merely to extend my boundaries. I'm willing even to blur their tracks so they expand if they can on their own.

I Centered

I yearn not to lock into any belief systems, including ideas about prayer. I wish to be open to my experience.

I Inward

An attempt at awareness can constitute, it seems to me, a form of prayer.

I Centered

Do I consider awareness and openness synonymous terms? Roughly so, yes. When resulting from openness, awareness can allow participation in the worlds of both knowledge and mystical experience.

I Outward

Judging myself an agnostic, I need eliminate nothing as untrue. All becomes possibility.

I Centered

The world in whole seems to me wide and open.

I Inward

...And I feel light. Full agnosticism brings me much joy.

I'm not required to prove the validity, even for me, of my experience.

I Centered

I understand that any terms I use don't define actuality. They only articulate my personal descriptions formed from my own inner searchings.

I Outward

And I fully concede that my categories erroneously divide the seamlessness of all consciousness, human and otherwise.

I Centered

I'm convinced that criteria and concepts are spawned entirely by humankind. They, unlike the process of conceptualization, don't constitute actuality. The what-is consists of those twin children of manifestation: occurrence and experience.

I Outward

Whether our beliefs are factually right or wrong they're valid for ourselves because they're we. As humans we cannot escape our heritage of experiential subjectivity. It's this, not facticity, that validates all idea.

I Inward

We're home free to think and feel whatever we can and do without proof of its objective authenticity.

I Outward

If Christianity's events aren't historically true, look at the creativity involved in their invention and propagation! Human resourcefulness and thought could be manifestations—and are—of the "God spirit."

I Inward

Christianity occurs within many persons, believers. Does it matter whether it all is congealed in the so-called actual, historical incidents? As inventions they're just as miraculous as the original occurrences that possibly represent actuality.

I Outward

All attempt to ascertain basic reality produces metaphor.

I Centered

As an agnostic I'm compelled to consider Christian icons and myths symbolically rather than literally. My job, then, is to determine the meaning which they hold for me.

I Outward

Their past and present actuality is irrelevant to them because I've only my interiority with which to weigh factuality.

I Centered

But I'm not stating to myself whether or not I judge Christian canons to be historically accurate. I simply don't know the "truth" of the case...

I Inward

...a standpoint that contents me.

I Centered

Yet perhaps the deity of the New Testament and my own at least somewhat can overlap.

My metaphorical interpretations are my personal projections. From what in me do they arise? Not only from the pool of what-is, from is-ness, but also from its source.

Irrefutable evidence is to my mind always at least somewhat unverifiable.

I Inward

I'm glad. If fully attainable it would rob us of the autonomy of choosing our commitments.

I Centered

The aim of any spiritual quest, it seems to me, should be experience, not the knowledge which to every meaningful degree is unprovable.

I Inward

Spirituality means what to me these days? Openness, awareness, and whenever possible foregoing the predetermination of setting temporary or long-range goals.

I Centered

Following that statement, I immediately express an aim: To become more and more nonjudgmental in reacting to all of life, particularly people.

I Outward

I don't wish to renounce my discriminations born of my preferences. I do, however, hope to appraise them less and less frequently as indicating right/wrong, good/bad, better/worse.

I Centered

I can't feel uniformly outgoing toward all people. I don't even wish I could. Not only are meanings of my emotional responses supplied for me by their differences, but these also seem to honor the uniqueness of their sources.

I Inward

Affectionate feelings toward a particular object appear to me to differ from the spirit itself of loving.

Yet these days, although I fear seeming sentimental, even unrealistic, I'm feeling loving of the world.

I Outward

Love, compassion, hopes and wishes for worldwide peace can radiate outward from a boundless heart-center, if you will, which each of us harbors.

I Centered

Every moment of my constant changing incorporates my entire history preceding it. I can claim no other continuity.

I Inward

If I'm the nonessential nonentity I believe myself to be, what or who is it that I find I am? My answer at moments of fulfillment and self-recognition is this: I manifest my own bit of oneness, voidness, awareness. In such times aspiration and yearning for more fall away. All is complete, as am I, and I exist not at all.

My views and feelings shift not just day to day but even hour by hour, or from one moment into the next.

I Centered

I refuse to chastise myself for changeability. Life, including my inner own, isn't and needn't prove stationary.

I Inward

My prescription for freedom and therefore joy is a waiting without pre-choice to discover whatever will happen.

4. MY THOUGHTS ON GOD

I Outward

God is for me the unknowable. The deity of my personal projections, however, is voidness contained within all phenomena. This emptiness is oneness, allness, fullness, stillness, the whole of manifestation.

I Inward

Perhaps my own god is included in God of the All.

I Centered

The divinity infuses all of my awarenesses.

I Inward

If so, I can claim a personal deity containing my theorizings. Because I find them difficult to relinquish I inwardly voice: Hoorah!

I Outward

I mull this issue: Why would God not create persons who freely choose "the good"?

First, the thrust within and from any possible deity, in my view, is entirely toward diversification. Yet criteria inherent in earthly creatures could occur only if objective to us "in space." And built-in proclivity in humans would demand of deity a standard exterior to people.

I Centered

All our human values of morality are numerous, conflicting and relative solely to us. We each create our shifting appraisals exclusive to ourselves. Among us persons, therefore, variety of belief and behavior results. Goodness, then, consists of what?

I Outward

Second, a requirement of cosmic multiplicity is human choice that's genuine. The license for it is essential to the evoking of complexity and variety among people, both individually and universally.

I Centered

Opportunity to evolve into, create and develop one's personal concept of what's good is basic to human autonomy.

I Inward

Inner growth occurs in open-ended freedom.

I Centered

Choosing confined to selection of any "only" is predetermined and consequently not impartial. Unbiased decision can occur solely if alternatives are not only viable but also equally available within oneself for weighing.

I Outward

To continue my conceptualizing: I'm an advocate in religious thinking of Process Theology.

I Centered

How can any omnipresent deity not occur indigenously within all that was, is and will evolve?

I Outward

Paradoxically, God is, I consider, both transcendent and immanent. The absence of either of these cpacities would "limit the limitless"—i.e., God.

I Centered

The case seems to me not that this ground, field, groundlessness of all being has been present from the commencement of the cosmos. Rather, it decidedly is itself that very beginning as well as its present and future. Some aspect of what-is, it seems clear to me, is eternal...

I Outward

...even if in itself it completely alters. And that very generativity is the emptiness which releases and infuses both potential and manifestation in whole.

I Inward

Shall I call it "God"? If and whenever I wish? Why not?

I Centered

I strongly believe this much: No demarcations between cause and effect, God and God's creations, are valid or even inherently existent in actuality.

5. MY THOUGHTS ON JESUS

I Outward

Jesus within his inner life held views of himself and his mission. Were they externally accurate?

I Centered

To know him we needn't derive the correct answer to the question. These visions of his, no matter whether true or false, would in either case equally constitute a portion of his interiority.

I Outward

It's Christ's perception of God's will for him, rather than his own choices, that he enacted. Clearly he believed divine direction coincided with fruition of his personal destiny.

I Inward

This surrender to "the way" is to me Taoist.

I Centered

It also is aspiration unexceeded, if not unparalleled, which he in addition evokes in others.

I Inward

And soul, whether or not it's actual, meaning active, in any one instant is in my view the aspiring aspect or facet of self.

I Centered

Was or is Jesus divine?

I Inward

I neither consider that I know, nor do I care how to answer the question.

I Centered

He was a truly insuperable man. Whether or not his resurrection historically occurred, it offers with his crucifixion an unsurpassed metaphor for transformation, transfiguration, following a death.

I Inward

...Decease of the old and the spent in us—in me.

I Centered

I personally can't believe Jesus is uniquely divine. Manifestation-in-whole, to my mind, doesn't and can't contain a destiny for Jesus external to his culture, contacts, results to him of his life. His unduplicated divinity very well may be actual, but if so it eludes my experience.

I Inward

Yet I can accept the Christian church as the vehicle keeping alive the meanings of Christ's life.

I Centered

For what else can I consider Jesus a metaphor?

I Outward

The humanization of God, certainly, but so are we all.

I Inward

Christ symbolizes for me an arising from the ashes of the old in which the phoenix of new form appears.

I Centered

The resurrection not of what has passed but of potential and then its birthing.

I Outward

Jesus also represents the primacy of individual innerness contrasting with the outwardness of conventional life and choices. Perhaps most primarily he enacts love.

I Centered

He nullifies personal boundaries among individuals and groups of people. The antithesis of prejudice, his brand of empathy annihilates all feelings of superiority. His message is decidedly nonviolence.

I Inward

Despite the example he provides, I'm unable to offer everyone warmth of affection. Toward almost all people, however, I can feel compassion...

I Centered

...which requires at least some sense of identification with another person.

I Inward

I only can hope compassion is a form of love.

I Outward

Christ also exemplifies standing for one's convictions.

I Centered

And he demonstrates the deathlessness of their validity for many of his followers.

I Outward

The Christian church embodies and continues the meanings Jesus holds for civilization, championing and preserving their vitality.

I Inward

His import for me personally is strongest if I consider his divinity is shared by all of us. I elect to view him as the human chooser of his decisions and course. I balk a bit at conceiving him mainly as an instrument of an impersonal and divinely mandated destiny.

I Outward

He certainly was directed by God but by his own vision of God. He apparently received no dictates from above.

I Inward

The significance Jesus holds for me isn't diminished in the slightest by my viewing him as totally human. Rather, my allegiance to him becomes enhanced by his triumphs as a person. Newly he seems totally real to me as a man, whether or not as his share of trinitarian divinity.

My feelings toward him are tender and protective.

6. MY THOUGHTS ON THE TRINITY

I Outward

My firm belief is this: The external factual veracity of all speculation is unprovable. Interpretations of data and evidence, and of their significance, invariably are subjective and individual.

I Centered

Even if they also are in actuality correct...

I Inward

...for myself my statement holds firm.

I Centered

Faith in the trinitarian deity would violate for me the integrity of my conclusion that knowing what is and isn't true is for everyone an impossibility.

I Inward

Only perhaps; I can't be certain that even this premise is accurate.

I Centered

Such a stand, nevertheless, requires of me that I decide my own metaphorical concepts of the Christian structure and issues it poses. My task in surveying both as part of present me is this: to open for enlargements of my sense of symbolic suggestions.

I Inward

I'm not obliged, however, to concern myself with their historical and literal authenticities.

My hope is that my belief nothing is necessarily so isn't a nonspiritual perspective.

Instead of with faith, I elect to go with trust in the yields of as much accessibility as I can attain.

I Outward

As present-day manifestations, the trinity is potentialities of individual experiences, not essences.

I Centered

Possibilities abound for assigning metaphorical meanings to members of the divine triad. Candidates I personally propose for consideration follow:

I Outward

In my own Christian framework God is to me: the unknowable, ineffable, Buddhist "sunyata" (emptiness); all that was, is and will be; and therefore is manifest; describable as the ground, field, groundlessness of being.

Holy Spirit, or Holy Ghost, gives contact with, and experience of, God where and as apparent to and for people. Perhaps this member of the triad appears not only in and for humans, but in everything that is. Possibly Holy Spirit is void's manifestation of itself...

...as is Jesus. He, too, represents particularity. He exemplifies and demonstrates the humanity of God, the personal aspects of the deity. He is the essence of love and of aspiration.

I'll express myself somewhat differently:

God is the unknowable; Holy Spirit is humankind's experience of, connection with, fathomable aspects of the divinity; Jesus is the human facets and face of God made evident.

I Centered

I shall further venture elaborating possibilities of relationship within the trinity.

I Outward

God: void; Holy Spirit: experience, or manifestation, of God; Jesus: humanization, or personal aspects, of God.

God: all that is, creation; Holy Spirit: birthing, Mary; Jesus: love.

God: androgyny; Jesus: maleness; Holy Spirit: femaleness.

God: the whole of what-is; Jesus: its articulation and exemplification; Holy Spirit: human experience of it.

God: unknowable, unspeakable mystery pervading all that is; Jesus: embodiment of, first, love, and, second, aspiration; Holy Spirit: sanctified mother, Mary.

I Centered

Some in-brief considerations follow:

I Outward

God, I repeat, is all that was, is and shall be. Jesus embodies not only love and aspiration but also dedication to personal destiny. The Paraclete fosters inner happening and creativity.

I Centered

I wish to tie in the trinity with my thinking I expressed earlier. In different words I'd postulated that the union of emptiness/manifestation embraced all experience. As a consequent stipulation I offer this condensed summary:

I Outward

God: emptiness; Jesus: manifestation; Holy Spirit: experience.

I Centered

According to biblical accounts Christ performed miracles but not, I note, in his own behalf.

Jesus exemplifies love in not claiming or attempting to prove identity as the Messiah. He thereby grants humans free choice of whether or not to believe his message.

I Inward

I've at times a sense of myself as a center in the heart of God, of Jesus and of the Holy Spirit-as-Mary.

The three then seem to me aspects of oneness.

My personal linkings to facets of the trinity obviously shift. Why shouldn't they? Definitions I offer of their characteristics are, at best, my own subjectivities.

When I feel connected with God, thanks to the Holy Spirit, I find myself feeling loving and enveloping toward Jesus and the entire world— including, frankly, myself.

7. MY THOUGHTS ON THE NONTRINITY

I Outward

The Madonna as Mary can be considered a manifestation of Holy Spirit. In this depiction she symbolizes the sanctity of birthing Holy Mother. She thereby incorporates fertility. Additionally, she personifies the wisdom of the goddess Sophia. Her knowing isn't dominantly intellectual but also embraces the psyche's sensory, emotional and intuitive functionings.

I Centered

These of her facets represent some of life's processes: creation and inner growth.

I Inward

I envision the energy of Madonna, because she incorporates wiseness, as more overarching than Mary's.

I Centered

Did God through Holy Spirit birth Mary? The deity perhaps transmitted creative power to her and love capacity into Jesus?

I Inward

The tenderness, protectiveness and love I feel toward Jesus is perhaps Mary within me. To find him in any one moment I needn't draw my image of him into the center of my chest. My heart reaching out to him stumbles against no boundaries.

I Centered

Birthing occurs as epiphany and concurrent resurrection whenever experience generates newness.

I Outward

As for the Buddha, Jesus and Mohammed, within their inner lives they held views of themselves and their missions. Which if any were externally accurate? We needn't obligate ourselves to probe for answers to this question.

I Centered

Their visions, no matter whether true or false, would in either case equally constitute their innerness. So to try understanding any or all of their messages we can content ourselves with honoring their own versions of themselves, words and works. As I've already suggested, to attempt sensing Jesus we need only accept his image of himself.

I Outward

The trinitarian god of Christianity makes possible a relationship no other religion provides between the human and the divine. Buddhism proffers a ground of being which doesn't incorporate divinity full-fledged. Sufism and Hinduism (and to my sparse knowledge, Mohammedism) offer a truly personal relationship with deity (or deities, in the case of Hinduism), as do religions glorifying the divine feminine or great mother. But none of these faiths provide the pathway to a god except through a teacher, guru or spiritual master not fully holy. Christianity differs from other religions by wedding the human and the sanctified.

I Centered

The personhood of Jesus is that of the divinity itself his resurrection signifies. Connection with either God or Christ gives simultaneously and with immediacy the pathway to the other.

I Outward

Jesus, the Buddha and Mohammed to me share the crux of their messages. Each of the three—the Buddha, with his compassion; Mohammed by his vision of one God of All; and Jesus, through his life and crucifixion—predominantly signifies love.

I Centered

Jesus renders suffering legitimate, validates it. Christianity in this respect differs from the Buddhism with which I'm familiar. Christianity, unlike Buddhism (exclusive of Zen) as I understand it, doesn't consider suffering inevitably the result of attachment springing from ignorance.

I Inward

If "Thou art the Buddha," a long-term sensing of mine, then "Thou art the Christ" and Mohammed also, as is everyone. Each of us "Thou"s partakes of the same universal energy and continues Buddha, Mohammed and Christ.

I Centered
I can sense I'm both a Buddhist and a Christian.
I Inward
Christmas at times signifies for me the rebirth of free will.
I Outward
Christmas in my thinking symbolizes birth itself; the crucifixion embodies death; and the resurrection incorporates rebirth...
I Centered
...possible only because preceded by the crucifixion.

8. MY THOUGHTS ON THE CRUCIFIXION

I Centered

For considering issues of the crucifixion I discover I personally must assume a deity both knowledgeable and directly involved concerning the cross. Results of my contemplations from this perspective appear below.

I Outward

If God caused or allowed the crucifixion as penance for his earlier misdeeds toward mankind, why? In what fashion does this sacrifice recompense his servants long dead? Do Jesus and/or God consider the death expiation of all evil past, present and future? In what way can one agent (even if divine) cancel the wrongdoing of another?

I Centered

Put differently, how does the crucifixion convert sin into sinlessness?

I Inward

In short, I can't accept that the payment for wrongdoing committed by God or humans could legitimize the crucifixion.

Nor can I consider that Christ died for our past, present or future evils.

I Centered

I concede, of course, that he perished because of the deeds of others. But I'd find difficulty in worshipping a deity who would commandeer into death even his own son. I also can't follow the logic of a divinity (whom I refer to here as masculine because Jesus named him "Father") who would condemn his own godliness in the person of his son to die in recompense for the evil of his subjects.

I Inward

Surely from God's standpoint Jesus was crucified for more cogent reasons.

I Outward

What if from God's standpoint Jesus had to undergo crucifixion in order to resurrect and thereby impart this message: "There is no death"?

I Centered

But what purpose of the deity would human and personalized immortality serve?

I Inward

I can't accept the premise that it occurs. The possibility contradicts my sense that emptiness means, in part, no permanent divisions.

I for myself feel no need to postulate individual eternalities, including my own.

I Centered

So what is my version of events which possibly transpired that brought Jesus to the cross?

I Outward

God to me is, and thereby allows, all that was, is and ever shall be. Occurrences, each following on another, precipitated Christ's fate. His responses to questionings by the Roman authorities were critical in sealing his doom.

I Inward

With utter courage he refused to compromise or betray the truth of his identity.

I Centered

In my view, he considered himself the prophesied Messiah.

I Outward

Christ didn't die for our sins. Rather, human evil murdered him. The crucifixion demonstrated our freedom of choice...

I Centered

...the curse or gift afforded by God to people.

Jehovah ceases biblical punishment to allow persons the consequences of their exercising free will. We are forced to become ourselves the gods of our own destinies. The deity is available for help when it's asked for, but now refuses to force his will on his creatures.

I Inward

Jesus by his example taught us to live with integrity and love. To counteract his message is to crucify God. The cross is the evil of ignoring God's edict posted through Christ.

I Outward

If Christ wasn't the recipient from God of supernatural capacities, he steadfastly lived and suffered results of actions he chose.

I Centered

Yet suppose God had bestowed on Jesus miraculous powers. Jesus might have prevented his being nailed to the cross or, once there, brought himself down from it.

I Outward

To perform either feat would have nullified human freedom to determine the consequences of actions.

I Centered

Christ's rationale for not attempting to circumvent his crucifixion possibly approximated this: "The message, not the man." He'd planted his seeds of wisdom. Now the choice of whether or not to cultivate them lay with others.

I Outward

If we assume a totally potent deity, perhaps the crucifixion is the price God paid for bequeathing free will to humans.

I Inward

If so, our legacy was an act of the deity's unsurpassed love for us.

I Centered

Its total givingness is underscored through our nonforfeiture of our self-determination and by God's nonintervention to save Jesus from the cross.

I Inward

We, too, remain free to accept or reject divinity as we choose.

I Outward

Not only humankind but the entire universe is blessed or cursed with self-determination. Results at times are extremely unwelcome.

I Centered

Jesus, for his part, was willing to be hanged so that through him God could exemplify total love: non-annihilation of human choosing.

I Inward

The triumph belongs to Christ and consists of his and God's willingness for Jesus to die in behalf of free will.

I Centered

Does Christ's crucifixion, resurrection and ascension denote a birth on God's part of compassion and forgiveness toward humans?

I Outward

Did the deity evolve into a new morality?

I Centered

Has the Jehovah of the New Testament renounced Old-Testament harshness and judgmentalism?

I Inward

Could the cross constitute God's penance for his earlier relationships with his subjects?

I Centered

Did Jehovah crucify himself through Jesus? Was he born again in the resurrection as God of Love?

I Inward

I've no firm answers, only my version of possibilities, to offer.

I Centered

Could God foresee the spread of Christianity resulting from the crucifixion and resurrection?

I Outward

If so, was this prescience the reason for permitting Jesus to hang from the cross? What did Jesus believe was God's purpose in allowing the death?

I Inward

Did he even concern himself with replies from either himself or God? Or was he satisfied merely with fulfilling his "father's" apparent plan for him?

I Outward

Did the deity exemplify self-love through loving the son in whom he was well pleased?

I Inward

These questions occur to me without my entertaining even opinions of their answers I can't possibly know.

I Centered

Isn't the burden of guilt for the death of Jesus the legacy of all past, present and future participants in whatever guise?

I Inward

How can we humanely spend it?

9. MY THOUGHTS ON THE RESURRECTION

I Outward
I'm assuming the possible actuality of the resurrection as my way of exploring its symbolic meanings below:

I Centered
The personhood of Jesus is that of the divinity itself his resurrection and ascension signify. Connection with either God or Christ gives simultaneously and with immediacy the pathway to the other.

I Outward
The resurrection trumpets "behold your deed." It demonstrates that incorruptibility and devotion cannot be annihilated. It announces an invitation to heed both God and son.

I Centered
Should we reject it and fail to care for one another, we could destroy humanity and also our planet. Each symbol is a metaphor for what else? Answers are individual for determination by each person.

I Inward
Does Christ's survival of death followed by his ascension carry this message? That no sin, not even the murder through his son's fate of God, is fatal or final?

For me, the cross implies a triumph over even seeming ultimate defeat.

I Centered
Is the deity promising life for the individual following physical death?

I Inward
I believe the answer to be yes.

I Centered

The resurrection signifies to me the immortality of the cosmic energy fueling us all. Our bodies partake of it, then die. Yet the manifest emptiness that generated us proceeds eternally.

I Outward

We resurrect, in my view, by rejoining the pool of celestial vibration that births each bit and whole. Our personal soul then belongs once more to the All.

10. MY THOUGHTS ON SIN

I Outward

The occurrence of evil is one price of our ingrained capacity to exercise our free will through choice.

I Centered

The difference between sin and evil, if any? My viewpoint is this: Sin primarily involves the internal self, whereas evil includes it but also affects the world.

I Outward

I define both as whatever impedes or thwarts the respect and autonomy rightfully due every human.

I Centered

The evil of self-righteousness under the guise of religion is an attempt to sanction and sanctify the unsanctionable and unsanctifiable: good/evil, right/wrong.

I Outward

Certainly much that is unconscionable has been propogated and promulgated beneath the banner of service to a "religious" cause.

I Centered

But institutionalized worship offers one answer to the spiritual longing in human nature for contact with divinity. Communal observance helps to supply form and meaning to aspirational seeking. Especially when not intolerant, it does sanction and sanctify human yearning to find and connect with the source of its existence.

I Outward

As for sinfulness, I consider it judgmentalism of myself and others. It enshrines appraisal it forgets is always subjective.

I Inward

And I don't believe that labeling as sinful any aspect of myself fosters tolerance of who I am. When I suffer self-blame I transfer my rejected aspects onto others. I then can't accept them as fully as I long to.

I Centered

"Sin" could serve to symbolize which candidates other than self-righteous intolerance?

I Outward

For an opening answer, not allowing the focus of my attention to register in my own mind what it exactly is; not respectfully responding to it as purely itself; coating it with my own ideas about it.

I Inward

Next, I readily might assume my resulting invention is the actuality...

I Centered

...which in my hubris I equate with the true occurrence I forsake...

I Inward

...failing to recognize my image of it as simply my own.

I Outward

This process leaves the world as it truly is essentially unknown.

I Centered

The sinfulness of the procedure lies where?

I Outward

First, in not acknowledging the abuse which revisionist receptivity imposes upon actuality. Second, in not attempting a vision progressively clearer.

I Inward

So let me enjoy what-is without attempting additions to it.

I Outward

What-is doesn't require fixing by me or need my garnishings of it, my arrogant inclements to it.

I Centered

These machinations occur, I suspect, nearly universally. They infuse the legacy of humaness I and others inherit.

I Outward

Yet I don't think we can blame the complexity and conflictedness of personality on one aspect of its manifestation.

I Inward

My job is only to recognize whatever occurs within me.

I Outward

A number of theologians consider "original sin" the fall from innocence of human identity into self-consciousness. Their perspective implies the nature of our redemption: rediscovery of our lost sense of oneness with the All.

I Centered

Regaining it doesn't require sacrificing comprehension of who we individually are. And uncontaminated awareness of phenomena allows us to experience both worlds: the particular and the mystical.

I Inward

It is thus, it seems to me, that we enlarge ourselves.

11. MY THOUGHTS ON PRAYER

I Centered

I've received a suggestion to "pray for faith." To whom or what? And with which goal in mind?

I Inward

How yearn toward that which I entertain no glimpse of? Shouldn't I need a vision giving me at least a hint of the believing I'm to pray that I attain?

I Centered

Wouldn't my wishing for faith imply I've in some manner already achieved it?

I Inward

I nevertheless find myself momentarily wishing to pray.

I Centered

To God? To Jesus? Either or both? To the Holy Spirit, in my view usually a feminine energy? And why this urge?

I Inward

I hope to communicate with parts of myself not available to me in any other way. I'm assuredly not ready to supplicate. I also want to acknowledge to my otherness—foci of my prayers—what I long for.

I Outward

I'll correct myself. My "otherness" seems an illusion. I'm a portion of All. A more accurate wordage is that which I already used: "parts of myself not available to me in any other way."

I Centered

Perhaps for me prayer would particularize in a unique fashion my sense of cosmic oneness.

I Inward

Possibly my conceptualzing and my meditatings are for me forms of prayer.

I Centered

I surmise that we pray not to persuade God to oblige us.

I Outward

Nor do we think to impart information about ourselves already registered by the All-knowing. Rather, we converse with the deity for this reason:

I Centered

We speak to a totally understanding listener (an irrelevance whether or not a projection of our own) to formulate that about ourselves which otherwise would remain amorphous.

I Outward

Briefly, we communicate with God to hear and so to learn what we think and feel.

I Centered

Prayer also ends our isolation and consequent loneliness.

I Inward

Shall I let myself pray if and when I wish to? I hope so.

III

CONFESSIONS OF MY MEDITATIVE SELF

1. MY EXPERIENCE IN AGNOSTICISM

I Outward

In differing contexts I previously express the viewpoint I espouse below. I wish my present statement also to stand alone. I'm not claiming it necessarily should prove valid for anyone but me.

I Centered

I realize in my bone marrow that my words and thoughts may bear absolutely no resemblance to actuality. Furthermore, I now accept— fully, I hope—my agnosticism, defined how?

I Outward

First, as the premise that every standpoint may or may not coincide in whole or in part with what-is. Second, that no method whatsoever avails for testing, measuring or ascertaining the external, objective validity of belief or its any portion.

I Inward

These perspectives permit me to adopt whichever theory or creed appeals to me. I shall do so on this understanding with myself: My concepts of the moment may or may not completely or partially mirror what perhaps is true.

I Centered

I now consider myself a true agnostic. I'm convinced (There! Already I'm contradicting myself!) absolutely no one can "know" whether any beliefs coincide with a reality other than their own occurrence.

I Inward

Accepting the impossibility of certainty, I no longer concern myself with the "truth" which I and no one can discover and that may not exist.

I Centered
I now neither agree nor disagree with any presented premise.

I Inward
"Can't-know" renders irrelevant the concern for whether belief is true or false.

"Can't-know" is the license for, and necessity of, believing whatever one pleases.

I Outward
Recompense for relinquishing the need to be "right": No idea can be proved "wrong." Acceptance of this premise opens the door to inner freedom: personal choice of viewpoint.

I Inward
"I don't and can't know" brings me a feeling of liberty. "I know" offers instead a sense of security, one which for me would prove narrowing and constrictive.

I don't want to lock myself into a permanent state, differing from "I don't know," of "I can't know."

I Outward
Unbelief, as definitely as any other philosophical or religious perspective, attempts to provide its host with security. All standpoints, including probably all possibilities of agnosticism, can prove constricting obstacles to full openness.

I Inward
I feel more at peace with a fully agnostic postion than with my attempts to formulate the nature of the cosmos. I can indulge my need to conceptualize when it again arises. But when I humor it, let me please remember this: Even my nerve endings now believe all is mysterious and miraculous because it exists at all.

I Centered
The glory for me in my agnosticism is its freeing me of trusting in any kind of thought structure or system—mine or anyone else's. It's a prize, long arriving, which I don't wish to relinquish.

I Inward
I newly feel more unburdened, lighter. My problems can become more fully those of everyday existence. Perhaps more importantly, I unleash myself to increase my connectedness with the outside world, including nature's display of wonders.

I Centered

We needn't diagnose nor label the meaning of our experience. We can't with any validity.

I Outward

Experience belongs to the mystery of what-is. Our inner happenings arise from the incomprehensible field, or groundlessness, of being itself.

I Inward

We can accept whatever meaning inner or outer event contains for us as our interpretation of it.

I Centered

But the validation of our experience lies in its occurrence and requires no other.

2. MY EXPERIENCE IN RENOUNCING

I Outward

The phenomenological world apprehended is to me not an illusion. It is merely a partial perception of reality. Nothing in any way perceivable manifests the whole of what is, but, rather, a portion of the unity of the All.

I Centered

The world experienced by our senses and minds is all reality, portions of its unity flowing one into the next with none more basic than any other.

I Outward

Nothing is a reflection of what-is because all simply is, in fact, is-ness, the "it."

I Inward

My thoughts, like those of everyone, are merely happenings, phenomena, in the whole of everything.

I Centered

Actuality is absolute as occurrence, manifestation. As my subjective experience it also is indisputable.

I Inward

Is my question, then, to what degree do my beliefs and other inner phenomena reflect universal is-ness?

I Outward

Reflect it? They're part of it. Manifestation creates them.

I Inward

I no longer wish to categorize my incidents of innerness as, say, imaging or pure awareness, intuition.

I Centered

None of it is superior or more "accurate" than some other incident; it's all just examples of phenomenalizing.

I Inward
Any inner event of mine creates its own actuality, as much manifestation as any others existent wherever. It perhaps even initiates a newness.

I Outward
All—everywhere—is the moment's episode. And every bit of it is empty.

I Centered
How much my experience of my own voidness corresponds with "objective reality" is beside the point.

I Outward
It constantly creates an "objective reality" of its own because it belongs to the cosmos.

I Inward
And I can never escape the happenstance that my own subjective perceiving is, in fact, inescapable as interiority, no matter the degree of "truth" it might reflect.

I Centered
Against what should I measure my inner transpirings? By which criteria? None whatsoever. I shouldn't...

I Inward
...and don't wish to rate myself at all, especially since I believe "objective reality" is unknowable with any certainty. In any and all cases it's, for me, my own inner life.

I Centered
When I needn't concern myself with the actuality, the factualness, of any imaging my thought evinces, I free myself to ruminate, even fabricate, however I please.

I Inward
Cogitating lies embedded in my nature. It invites in me new associations. If I let myself refrain from aiming to establish any veracities I can play—yes, play—as much as I please with my conjecturings.

They're who I am, my method of functioning. I relinquish my attempts to invalidate my ponderings.

I Outward
I previously recorded the credo I now reaffirm: All is the self-manifestation of unbounded emptiness.

I Centered

I don't know and in no way can ascertain whether this postulation or some other—mine and anyone's— expresses even a single actuality.

I Outward

All concept is a grasping for nonexistent fixity. Nothing transpires to clutch that isn't an effort at hanging on to what isn't: a permanent fixedness.

I Inward

That belief, too, is another subjective reaching for, attempt to create and establish, a stability that isn't: the stability of nonstability.

I Outward

Holding a focus is only another attempt at a permanence that's merely a mirage.

3. MY EXPERIENCE IN HOSPITALIZATION

I Outward

Hospitalized by a bout of atrial fibrillation, I lie after midnight alone in a blackened room.

I Inward

It seems to me a definite possibility that I might die.

I Centered

I intuit this:

Life and death constitute a single and boundless sphere. Within it they occur as a front-back continuum. Only a membrane separates the two. This film is thin, nonobstructing, permeable, transparent and transmutable.

I Outward

For each of us life and death oscillate in an unimpeded flow through the scrim separating them. Every large and small ending gives rise to the next beginning until, at last, we exit from bodily habitation. At this point the membrane finally has been pierced. Here on earth personal cycling between the two related states ends.

I Inward

My feelings concerning whether I live or die are both accepting and impersonal.

Were I to leave earth tomorrow it's okay with me. All vestiges of yearning to cling to my physical continuance dissipate.

I now, perhaps paradoxically, greatly enjoy my daily living and relish the content of my hours.

I Centered

In different words, I'm detached about whether I live or die but involved emotionally to the full in the actualities of my existence.

I Inward

I'm sighting death as white: absence of all color. Life, in its essence, I oddly view as black: mixture of all hues. Other tints, like their sources, are partial.

I Centered

Do masks speak of death?

I Outward

Maybe partially, as its archetypical representations.

I Inward

I love masks, especially African, possibly because on the whole they're of dusky wood. I sense they depict for me my dark side and my primitive self.

I Outward

They also paradoxically and simultaneously hide what they bare. Their very simplicity evokes projections actualizing a viewer potential or two...

I Centered

...including my facets I sometimes ignore.

I Inward

Often when I'm in bed at night and attempting to relax, all my perceptions seem to rise from a realm of blackness, silence, stillness. Their source shows itself as a tunnel, or funnel, from which, still unformed, all appearancy occurs. Its sphere of origin is light.

I Centered

Allegorically, the darkness is emptiness. The brightness, almost white, yields manifestation.

I Outward

I don't suggest, however, that phenomena lie in blackness beyond the range of void. Both blackness and whiteness are aspects of the blending of emptiness and manifestation.

I Centered

In actuality they depict my personal experience of the dark and light of my own consciousness, and no more.

I Inward

I feel as if I'm reflecting in a small and restricted manner the cosmic field of being.

I Centered

But all of us exemplify it every moment of our living.

4. MY EXPERIENCE IN BELIEVING

I Inward

I acknowledge that theorizing is one of my most enjoyable and exciting modes of being. Nevertheless, concepts are merely my subjectivity. I wish to avoid jeopardizing the primacy of my experience—emotional, intuitive and perceptual—with intellectualizing.

I Centered

I could relinquish my lifelong search for an elusive but presumed-existent truth of my own...

I Outward

...which—now my conviction is—doesn't exist.

I Inward

My commitment to "maybe so, maybe not" concerning any and all belief frees me from an endless chase of ephemeral revelation.

I become at liberty to explore without goal or a sought result.

I Centered

So why seek any knowledge at all of that which basically is?

I Inward

In the hope of connecting with as much of it as our fragmentary being states allow.

I Centered

I might postulate I'm free to believe whatever I wish. To some extent the claim is true. But here's my actual case: What am I able to adopt as an opinion while I maintain intellectual integrity? I can't push aside what seems to me to be fact, or even truth, to satisfy a preference for a particular opinion.

I Inward

So I'm not truly free to invest my allegiance wherever I'd like. Even if I could ignore my mind's misgivings, a deeper part of me would remind me, if I listen to myself, that I'm pushing doubts aside. I believe as I do, even if I'd prefer otherwise. Let me remember to value as much honesty of avowal as I can manage and tolerate.

I Centered

My focus at present has shifted from the content of beliefs to attitude toward believing. The perspective I'd like to foster in myself is one of non-appraising: the understanding of evaluating as merely "my stuff," as is this thought concerning it. Humans produce "stuff" which is they but to me not judgeably reflecting "the way things are." And this view of mine also is only "my stuff," as are all my ideas, feelings, sensings, including those occurring in my meditatings.

I Inward

The labels "oneness," "allness," "voidness," "manifestation" feel to me descriptive of truth. But they, as thought, are only my metaphorical assumptions, subjective experience.

I Outward

My cogitations, nevertheless, belong as much to the whole of phenomena as do anything else. Their mere existence grants them their right to occur.

I Centered

I consider my job is to interpret for myself the meaning of symbols which present themselves to me.

I Inward

Yet I'm convinced I don't know actuality even if I persuade myself otherwise. I can't escape my subjectivity. It is I, and I'm unable to judge my thoughts apart from it.

Even my pushing, prodding and pressing myself, when it occurs, I'll accept as okay—"for now." I'll try to forego rejecting what doesn't fit my preconceptions. I'll attempt to allow uprisings in me, then decide among them when they require choice or action.

I Centered

My own experience is never a totality of its source or of its aspect singular or plural. Voidness, oneness, thereness I can resonate only as I.

I Inward

I accept that I consist of changing subjectivity. So I'm left with no alternative to following my impulse and bent of the moment.

I Centered

Other than these, what do I find in me to trust?

5. MY EXPERIENCE IN METHOD

I Inward

When I'm graced with a state of experiencing oneness/emptiness, what is it I've managed to do?

I Outward

I'm at present inclined to adopt a procedure of merely paying attention to my inner and outer scenes of each moment.

I Centered

I of today can think of no preferable method of experimenting. And of course any plan of mine is always open to my revising.

I Inward

I tune my awareness—my seeing and hearing— without imaging but only perceiving—to what? My self: body, emotions, thoughts, but especially my physical being. I manage not to establish mental boundaries between me and all else. In my "just looking" I include my own body, but only that of it which my senses perceive.

If I want to see what I'm watching as it actually is, it's important to spare it my projections.

I Centered

What do I mean by projections? Images coming from my own subjectivities, which never are really separate from the entirety of life.

I Outward

Projections come from what-is, which arises from its source: the unknowable behind it. This unfathomable shows itself in these externalizations of mine...

I Centered

...affording me opportunity to experience (though not understand) my part of the cosmic whole.

I Inward

The "I" of today meditates with a sense of non-involvement in my surroundings and my own processes. But I don't wish to live on a plane of constantly not investing in either one, of unrelieved withdrawal and impersonality. I accept my attachments, especially to my emotions, as enrichments of my existence.

I Outward

What in me never changes? To borrow from T.S. Eliot: the point of my turning world. In other words, cosmic evincings that like all else I invariably and always am. But my absorption of this energy isn't really a "point." It's a diffusion, rather, throughout myself.

I Centered

And "myself" is what? My total processes in the moment. They alter by the minute. No permanent, unchanging inner entity, therefore, exists.

I Inward

Are my nuclear and observing selves the same?

I Outward

Their edges touch one another's boundaries but their centers are discrete.

I Inward

Is my observer the same as my acting person?

I Outward

Yes and no. They're different phases of a single unity.

I Inward

Rather than my witnessing side, detached, I'm emphasizing my experiential part: awareness without separation. No two-part "me" or personality.

I Centered

And no way of experiencing my body is superior to any other. I needn't strive for a sense of transparency, lightness or the like...

I Outward

...for the belief is fallacious that achieving it would usher me closer to contact with cosmic reality.

I Inward

So let me acknowledge that such effort is futile.

I Outward

Whatever bodily awareness turns up in me at any one moment is manifestation of a universal force which doesn't discriminate "better" or "poorer."

I Centered
My identity is the totality of my every moment's conscious awareness and is therefore constantly changing.

All my ideas are projective subjectivities, my personal metaphors. And the same statement is applicable to everyone.

I Inward
Often I wish to focus my attention as fully as possible elsewhere than on myself.

I Centered
Truly to see a target of my attention I must drop my concern for its connection to me. It neither needs nor registers my apprehension of it.

I Outward
I recall advice of Alan Watts: "Don't try to do anything with it." I lose my perception of "the thing in itself" unless I refrain from all effort to bond with it.

I Centered
For my experiencing it's especially important not to attempt "filling the space" between me and what I'm looking at with any imagined or actual aspects of my consciousness. In other words...

I Inward
...I mustn't try to "feel oneness," call on awareness or connect with emptiness. If I don't strain to fill the void, but just look and listen...

I Outward
...emptiness will be apparent "all on its own."

I Inward
I abandon effort to connect with sunyata, the void. I now can sense and attune to emptiness without struggling for the experience.

A stance of mere readiness feels to me airy and expansive. I can give myself liberty to seek without goal or a sought result. I've dropped a burden.

Awareness of my inner emptiness is my most reliable route to ecstasy.

I Centered
It's best available by openness without any addition whatsoever.

I Inward
All of my feelings, no matter how painful, seem to me to be gifts from life.

6. MY EXPERIENCE IN STRIVING

I Inward
I find myself reaching, pressing, pushing for an undefined experience. Of what?

I Centered
Am I wanting connection at will with emptiness, oneness, consciousness, thusness/suchness—singularly, alternately or simultaneously?

Would I prefer the goal of impartiality to my conception of possibilities for inner occurrence?

I Outward
Shall I attend to which of my worlds: external or internal? Or should I rotate my focus between them?

I Inward
Am I anxious because I'm undecided concerning which of all my perceived alternates to opt for?

I Centered
How can I decide where I now wish to aim?

I Outward
This much I'm certain of: In my procedures I long to assign belief, theory, method a role as minimal as possible.

I Centered
I hope I forego any striving to replicate then meaningful but now former incidents. I shall attempt to view each experience as unique.

I Inward
I'm aware of an inner conflict. I reach and press for former awarenesses, fearing they'll disappear forever if I lose touch with them. Yet I also wish to let it all go if its unobstructed course is to leave.

I Centered
The more I cling to repetition of previous happening, the more firmly I crowd out whatever is new perhaps attempting to emerge.

I Inward

I also long to forego traveling down any pre-chosen track, even one of my own devising.

I Outward

As I mentioned earlier, Alan Watts advises, "Just look without trying to add anything."

I Inward

Attempting to apply his instruction helps me clear and clean out my psychic pores. But I don't plan prodding myself to "just look." Whatever happens I hope to let be.

I Centered

My issue seems to be: What amount of effort, if any, is commensurate with increase of openness? How much programming augments inner expansion or to what extent possibly impedes it?

I Inward

I confess I'm weary of striving for inner growth. One facet of me longs to relinquish all struggling for my betterment.

Yet I fear in part that if I wholly forego my seeking nothing within me will transpire.

I Centered

Were I to follow this impulse toward a letting go, a second voice within me warns I may become...what? A vacant glob?

I Inward

I long to slough off, move beyond, struggling for a certain type of interior happening. I want to follow my bent of each moment, or even allow myself a lack of direction. I crave just to live—which is all I've ever done anyway!

I wish to stop adding to my perceptions of "self" and/or "other."

I Outward

I attempt to enlarge them with meaning or some element of my reactions I consider is lacking. I reach and press in all inner directions when my experience seems inadequate for matching its potential. It's then that I muffle and kill occurrence altogether.

I Centered

Question: Why, then, do I quest at all? I remind myself: I hope to enlarge my connections with more and more of manifestation-in-whole.

I Inward

As a present concession to all my voices I'll proceed in this fashion:
I give myself liberty to explore, but without goal or a sought result.

7. MY EXPERIENCE IN RELEASE

I Centered

A strong aspect of my nature is my reaching for objectives. Yet I yearn to quiet myself as best I can and merely invite a state of availability to visit me. I also shall try to attempt neither managing its course nor assessing results.

I Outward

I shall shift my focus away from directing myself toward a goal I select. I now will transfer my efforts to an encouraging of my inner processes. I intend not to reach toward the future and possible attainment there. Instead, I'll fully involve myself in the present, aware, I hope, of its content and richness.

I Centered

I'm today inclined to adopt a procedure of merely paying attention to my inner and outer scenes of each moment. In this hour I can think of no more preferable method of experimenting. And of course any plan of mine is always open to revision.

If, as I firmly believe, judgments stemming from reasoning aren't infallible, my hunches must yield the answers for me to my inquiries.

I Inward

I'm eager to drop my attempts to attain a pre-selected realization or experience by using awareness of manifestation. I furthermore want to renounce my efforts at formularizing and jelling inner happening. Ensuring its never-failing accessibility and repetition is for me invariably futile.

I Centered

Shall I try opening to my own personal emptiness and/or thusness, then allow happening that's unguided (I hope!) to "take it from there?"

I Inward

Do I wish to forego and relinquish—whatever?

I Centered

I want availability to possibility which I assume only openness to my innerness can grant. Would achieving it require a full passivity which sacrifices all aim or goal? To what extent are objectives the prerequisites of inner expansion? Is true relinquishment of striving feasible? I'm reminding myself that even choosing to meditate counteracts goalessness or full passivity. In itself it can constitute a purpose.

I Inward

In answer, I shall attend to my urge to free myself from any programming of my meditation. I'm no longer willing to lock myself into pursuit of a particular kind of experience, spiritual or otherwise.

I Centered

Who can foresee or control the advent of rapture? Stimuli and their consequences differ as occasions shift. I doubt it can reappear from my struggling to relate with what lies beyond my body.

I Inward

I discover that ecstasy visits when I sense my personal emptiness in its manifestion of me. I doubt if it can arrive from my struggling to relate with what lies beyond me. And I learn a sense of exaltation is best available without my attempting any additions whatsoever in any realm.

I Outward

But jubilation can arise from the realness of everyday living.

I Inward

I long to shake off more than restrictions imposed by beliefs I adhere to. I crave escaping all structure, obligation, imperative which commitment to creed or concept involves.

I hereby choose to freefloat with whatever arises within me and not attempt to predetermine results.

I Outward

Directly above I frequently employ these convenient societal conventions: "I," "me," "my."

I Inward

I now allow within myself a sense of my emptiness; the mirage of my separateness from all else dissolves. "I" no longer exist.

IV

CONFESSIONS OF MY PSYCHOLOGICAL SELF

1. BASIC BELIEFS

From our births until our deaths we all are philosophers. We experience happenings and our own responding emotions. We observe. We strive to make sense of life, learn what behaviors assure our surviving and our attaining what we want. So we infer the nature of our world and the people in it.

As a requirement of this process we seek cohesiveness and consistency through our conclusions, conscious and unconscious. Consequently, the qualities we assign to the cosmos and its aspects attain within our psyches importance relative to one another. These projections of attributes onto the world and universe we awarely and unawarely shape into axioms that cluster in various depths around issues central to existence. Deductions stemming from and pointing toward these Basic Issues (BI's) function as our Basic Beliefs (BB's).

Owned or disowned, these bottom tenets of our philosophies mold and motivate our subsequent opinions, attitudes and feelings. They shape our goals and choices. As major conditionings of our traits and life styles, our inner visions of How Matters Stand sculpt the persons we are and will become. Throughout our lives they supply the meanings existence has for us.

Persons perhaps are, broadly speaking, of two kinds: those who crave the security they hope protection by the universe will offer them; and others who long for freedom even at its levied cost of uncertainty. I refer, of course, to major thrusts. No one dwells solely in either camp. Choice between these life arenas, nevertheless, strongly influences which BB's one adopts and retains.

The tone of Basic Beliefs (BB's) is far more emotional than cognitive.

I suggest that the tackling of opinions and suppositions piecemeal is haphazard and generally inefficient. If a premise fundamental to an entire inner construct is undermined or reinforced, the total structure of thought and feeling it supports can topple or toughen.

I offer below a perspective of bedrock assumptions. Adherence, recognized or not, from among its alternatives occurs universally. My schemata, like any, is entirely personal.

Primary Basic Beliefs

1. The cosmos is: (A) purposeful; or (B) experimental; or (C) unintentional.

2. The cosmos is: (A) hostile; or (B) neutral; or (C) benevolent.

3. The cosmos is: (A) knowable; or (B) equivocal; or (C) inscrutable.

Nearly all statements are of course phraseable as queries. Mine follow.

2. BASIC QUESTIONS

Basic Beliefs (BB's) convert readily into Basic Questions (BQ's).

BQ Amplifications
1A. Is the cosmos purposeful?

Does the cosmos contain within itself a direction in which it moves?

Is any course the universe takes instilled within it, or imposed upon it, by a deity other than the universe itself?

Is cosmic energy goal-propelled?

Can the universe exist for effecting a purpose pre-existent to it, either its own or one imposed upon it by its creator?

Is cosmic purposefulness, if existent, pointed toward the attaining of either unity or diversity?

Might cosmic aims, if such there be, conflict?

Do persons constitute a goal, or the goal, of the universe, or do they instead effect a goal or goals?

1B. Is the cosmos experimental?

Does the universe develop direction and purpose in the course of its constant changing?

Does the universe shift its path or paths, reinvent the end or ends toward which it gropes, along with, and also by means of, its evolving?

Is any purpose the cosmos now manifests single or multiple?

Do values exist as only human judgments?

Is purpose a conglomerate development of the cosmos rather than a predetermination?

1C. Is the cosmos unintentional?

Is manifestation of any kind self-evoked or self-achieved?

Might every happening as readily not have occurred?

Are all universal forces in essence entirely non-intelligent?

Is cosmic direction contained within each of its material manifestations?

Are both life and personhood mere happenstance?

Is purposefulness simply a path down which human development meandered?

Do valuings, concepts of ethics and virtues, not exist except within the brains and minds of people?

Are humans free to create the world of their choosings?

Does credit or blame for outcomes on earth belong strictly to its creatures?

2A. Is the cosmos hostile?

Is the universe so constituted that "Might makes right" with "the mightiest" status always elusive?

Does survival demand that one attain and maintain an ever-slippery control, or be controlled to one's disadvantage?

Is dissolution the end result of all change?

Is life a perpetual attempt to stave off the ravages wrought by the passage of time?

Does a goodly measure of catastrophe constitute the dole from "the Fates" to all creatures including persons?

Do the "laws" of a cruel Nature govern the universe?

Does Destiny destroy those whom it first elevates?

Are transgressions against cosmic requirements punished by the infliction of disaster on all culprits?

Is the universe hostile to only some living entities for reasons unknown to them which they are powerless to affect?

2B. Is the cosmos neutral?

Is whatever happens in the universe the product of mere chance?

Can life prove to be what each of its creatures manages to make of circumstances?

Does no predisposition exist toward either propitious or unfortunate event?

Is all merely what-is, and every judgment concerning it a product of subjective interpretation?

Can human being provide no focal point of the universe because there is none?

Is occurrence inherently irrelevant to its effect on living entities?

Are some persons fortunate and some unfortunate not because of any fateful predetermination exterior to them?

2C. Is the cosmos benevolent?

Is basic energy inherently nurturing of its manifestations?

In the cosmic scheme of operation, is the individual sacrificed only in behalf of a necessary wide survival?

To a degree, is fortuitous opportunity the legacy at birth of every living creature?

Might some persons be earmarked by powers not theirs for good fortune?

Are those people not "darlings of the gods" at least not divine whipping posts?

Is a desirable destiny achievable in good measure by one's own efforts?

Are unhappy occurrences often challenges that strengthen when met?

Do black hours in human lives frequently prove to be to some degree "the darkness before the dawn"?

Is misery quite often the consequence of human failure, hence the price persons pay for their freedom of willing and choosing?

Does the gift of life itself prove the bountifulness of the universe?

Is the power to love a caress from a caring cosmos?

3A. Is the cosmos knowable?

Is the energy, or its source, that governs the universe self-revealing?

Can persons directly connect with or comprehend, through reason, intuition or receptivity, basic energy or its source?

Might messages from whatever deity that may exist reach willing receivers?

Will people prove capable, as their learning increases, of understanding nearly all that is?

Are ethics and standards pertaining to human living either nonexistent, self-evident or revealed?

Is selection by universal forces, if ever occurring, of any persons for good fortune a recognizable beneficence?

Can ill luck be divined, hence circumvented, in advance of its occurrence?

3B. Is the cosmos equivocal?

Is the energy, or its source, that governs the universe at times or in some ways self-disclosing, while in other periods or aspects it remains disguised?

Do messages which circumstances send to humans seem readable on occasions, and at different times appear unfathomable or nonexistent?

Does the degree of transparency the universe manifests in any of its modes depend upon the seeker, the sought, or both?

Are at least some facets of reality destined to remain shrouded forever in mystery?

Is human knowledgeability limited even potentially in its capacity for comprehension of the nature and workings of the cosmos?

Might basic reality prove unpermeating of all that is, hence partially not present for discovery?

Do differences in viewpoint reflect the misinterpretable nature of phenomena?

3C. Is the cosmos inscrutable?

Is agnosticism the only attitude which is philosophically and/or religiously justifiable?

Is whatever energy that may source or govern the universe hidden and indiscernible?

Are the basic nature and fundamental workings of the cosmos undiscoverable?

Are lacks in human knowledge of the universe those of inadequacies of information, many of which are even potentially insurmountable?

Are ethics and standards which may govern all human living either nonexistent or unfathomable?

Is selection, if ever occurring, by universal forces of any persons for fortuitousness an unrecognizable beneficence?

Can misfortune never be divined, hence circumvented, in advance of its occurrence?

Do differences in viewpoint reflect the undisclosing nature of phenomena?

Other issues pertaining to BB's await.

3. BASIC ISSUES

My term for the fundamental dilemmas which living poses is Basic Issues (BI's). I discuss them as if each were a dual-sided coin or disk. I present both halves of all as I conceive them to be.

BI Content

Insignificance/meaning

isolation/inclusion

death/life

My wording of this final BI is so overarching that I'll particularize the imports which in my view it holds:

termination/continuation—more containing than the pairing of my third BI above;

groundedness/freedom—expressing the psychological dilemma induced by this issue;

essentialness/nothingness—suggesting self-boundaries experienced, respectively, as definitive or permeable;

and, most pointedly of all,

stability/flux—describing my version of the contrasting and basic characteristics of death/life.

BI's and BB's Linkages

BB's constitute our responses to BI's and our tools for coping with them. BB's serve as both strategists and stratagems of our survival.

At our births the universe becomes for all of us our versions of our circumstances. Totally uninterpreted by us, the cosmos of our personal scenes would consign us to full helplessness in dealing with BI's they pose. Our anxiety would prove absolute. By construing with our BB's we spare ourselves such unsustainable terror. Without them we of necessity would retreat into the lesser horror of insanity.

If the universe is purposeful it is meaningful; if benevolent it will include us in its offered bounties of belongingness; if knowable we can ground ourselves with our understanding of its principles of operation.

With such convictions as these we dispose of the possibilities that insignificance of the universe is real; that our home, the cosmos, will not invariably cherish us; and that death in its many guises, including the ultimate termination of our physical aliveness, does occur.

BB's also may result from a sense of us humans that the negative face of a BI shows us reality, with its positive shadow-opposite existent as mere projection of our wishful thinking. We then would postulate, although probably not as conscious conclusions, a cosmos experimental or unintentional, hostile or neutral, equivocal or inscrutable.

Circumstances shift. Life can seem to any of us meaningful in some ways; suggestive only of insignificance in others. Today's sense of isolation can flow into tomorrow's enjoyment of inclusion. The freedom, especially of choice, afforded us persons by our sense that our subjectivity conditions our perceptions and convictions can dissipate. Then the outer world once more lays claims to our focus. And death of one project, or relationship, may give rise to a rebirth: start of another creativity or personal connection.

Implications of Death/Life

As infants first gulping air we faced the BI most fundamental and pervasive of all: death/life. Our survival depended upon our breathing quickly. In existing outside a womb we continued relying on other persons for supply of all our needs, including reassurance that care of us would prove forthcoming. We promptly were confronted by, or let's say we confronted, the BI of isolation/inclusion by others. The then-current meaning or insignificance of life was that of whether or not it continued for us at all. As older children the question, largely covertly, arose: were we loved enough to be nurtured and so could survive.

As adults we often regard situations of daily life not merely as matters requiring decisions. We view them as portents and symbols pertaining to intimate relationships and foundational ways of life. We are sensitized, often unknowingly, to the permanence and pervasiveness of BI's.

Aloneness evokes in our memories of the child we once were its threat to our even existing. Too, only through relationship with others can we use and develop our human faculties, capacities and potentialities. These blocked, we suffer a multitude of painful mini-deaths. Our separateness also reminds us we will experience our own physical extinguishments in inner isolation.

If we're at the mercy of happenstance we can't assure our "full-term" survival. We try to reduce the risks which our vulnerability to chance occurrence poses. We struggle to know, to reassure ourselves of our knowledge, in order to predict outcomes. We hope we then can take measures to circumvent happenings we consider undesirable and to induce whichever we think we would prefer.

These efforts, to prove successful, require that we perceive, even obtain, a stable universe. In part, at least, we crave the ultimate stolidity which only changelessness could afford us. We forget that an unmoving cosmos would stagnate, atrophy into nonexistence. We overlook the consequence that our endeavors to survive threaten the very continuance we employ them to insure.

In actuality the universe, inclusive of ourselves, isn't fixed but fluid. In all its aspects change is the order of the day.

Our wiser recourse seems to be acceptance of outer and inner flow of eventfulness. We're free to trust that our human instincts and spontaneities will provide us adequate responses. Whatever impedes this process of reaction—in particular, adherence to strict, external imperatives; critical self-judgments—functions in behalf of a stationary order of consequent decay.

Challenges of BI's

Must we concede our victimization by an isolating and insignificant cosmos which rewards us for our travails only by ultimately killing us? The answer I profess is "No."

Person by person we can and do deal with BI's. Our world is repository of innumerable meanings, all of which we individuals, one by one, create. With the micro universes that we are, in our own behalfs we flip over, transform, the macro cosmos of totality: The Way Matters Stand. Our agents of empowerment are our conscious choices and commitments yielded to us by our BB's. These last, through our awareness of their actuality, we can reappraise, perhaps reaffirm. We at least unstintingly could accept them as core of our innerness from which our decidings arise in all their potency.

Our rescue from nihilism waits inherent in our human nature. We are blessed/cursed—-depending on our viewpoint—with inwardness. We live, and live through, our feelings, thoughts. We act. Most crucially, we choose, defaultingly or awarely.

Thus do we salvage and construct our freedom, acknowledged or not, from the fetters of automatism, happenstance. With the "positive" of personhood we answer the "negative" of impersonality: outerness, and the generality, universalness, of cosmos.

Yes, we will die. Until our deaths we can and do live. If the meaning of life isn't life itself, what is it?. Ours is the right to harken to each moment of our "hereness" as living's gift to us.

4. SURRENDER

Sellout

When we were infants our needs required another human for fulfillment. Frustration, in its moment of occurring, spoke to us of an unfriendly universe. Satisfaction attained instructed us in how to avoid the world's malice and succeed at gaining its beneficence. We began to learn the secondary power of mandatory pandering. The primary potency of our wishes, their expression as feelings, had for the while to be put aside. Our locus of attention shifted from ourselves to our scenes beyond us. As we aged, the process, continually reoccurring, gained force. More of our energies became invested outside our psyches than within them.

Two types of admonition prevailed to which we growing humans were compelled to harken: (1) specifications by other persons; (2) resultant disciplinary strictures imposed from within. Some rules belong in both categories. Both sets of regulations imply at least to some extent that the meaning of our lives is our significance not to ourselves but to others. In respect to BB's, those outer and inner dicti which we dare not modify speak to us of a cosmos hostile because purposeful at our expense, and surely knowable that our alibis for not observing its instructions are invalid.

Extent of Sellout

For the growing girls or boys we were, two inquiries capsuled the main criteria of how to respond to circumstances. They are: "What's better for me?" and "What smooths my dealings with others?" To bypass the first for full focusing on the second indicates a sellout which was deep. We youngsters asking the second question felt, and were, less compromised internally if our purpose was obtaining answer to the first. Fortunate were we sons or daughters whose lives allowed the honoring of our own welfares to prove primary.

Sense of Helplessness

As children we may have judged our caretakers incompetent to sustain us. At times, surely, any and all of them confronted us with their hostility. In either or both of these situations, our helplessness and the fear of it were our gravest threats, causing our deepest terrors. To avoid such distress we suppressed our anger about our predicament, unconsciously choosing instead to feel guilty. Better to blame ourselves for difficulties and disasters. We'd reform, and matters could thereby be righted. In this way we denied to ourselves that frustrations of our needs occurred beyond our realm of control, and that rejections of us were born of malice toward us.

We also bought the requisite belief that we were flawed. We embarked upon a series of maneuvers I describe below. These were designed to avoid, compensate for or overcome our assumed faults.

The relinquishment of our feelings, and ultimately their denial, constitutes our most basic and extensive sellout.

Choice

A sense of choicelessness obviates for us the necessity for further self-justifications. It grows from our acceptance that the rule, standard, truth pertinent to any moment is a given condition of being in this world, not to be transgressed.

Our deliberate choosing requires our attention to our own wants. When we consciously decide, we by implication acknowledge ourselves as rulers of our destinies. We function as our own gods. And for our hubris we may fear retribution from a named or nameless source. Pride comes in many packages and, as we've all been taught, goes before a fall.

We bravely can concede we create our source of choice through our self-accepted standards. In favor of standing erect we forfeit pillars—principles or persons—to lean on. We become free to recognize that none of us can fail to choose, and, like it or not, from within ourselves.

Control

Our sense of impotence readily can breed a drive to attain a control which, no matter its type or target, is always illusory. A sole exception: Our choices, aware or not, are invariably under our own dominion.

We strive to strike bargains with The Fates and hope that, by acting as if they're in effect, we succeed. Such negotiations are one-way affairs. No means exist of our unilaterally obligating the outside world to act in our behalf. Our inner sufferings lack all power to appease contingencies.

Our sellout of our innerness would seem to derive from this policy: Take charge of "out there." We then depend for our success on circumstances and other persons. These we never can fully influence. They remain in themselves contributory to our effect on them.

Judgment

Often the tool of control we reach for is "good judgment." We construct it from standards we consider to be impersonally and universally valid. We assume it will inform us accurately how we should feel, think and behave to affect the world beyond our skins in the manner we desire. Our conclusions, we hope, will divulge to us the ways we can or ought to expect our environment will present itself. We trust such deductions to afford us effectiveness in inducing coveted results within our external scenes. These judgments reassure us we actually know: who we are, how the world is, and therefore the ways we can transform ourselves, others and everything else, into that which all should be.

Evaluating "objectively" begins with our believing that guideposts we use for our task are valid independently of, apart from, us people. Resultant assessments can seem to offer us a true antidote to our sense of helplessness. In reality they ensnare us in a web of captivity to shoulds we manufacture. Our sole rescue from this impotence to which we consign our wills is our own subjectivity: those choices we base on what we are and wish for.

Shoulds

Our society hoists its shoulds on us, and we, in turn, adopt them. We may bypass acknowledging and examining them. We then project them as and onto whatever standards our own egos confirm and possibly further shape. "Standardized," our shoulds dictate our choices. Our rules, transforming our yardsticks into admonitions, insist we meet, even obey, our inner dictates. Primary among tools of the sellout, these injunctions serve it unfailingly. In actuality, their single sanction is our belief in their validity.

Standards and Criteria

We may fail to acknowledge that our standards, our criteria, are no more nor less than our own utterly personal beliefs. Undeniably we inherit many if not most of our opinions and convictions. But our accepting or rejecting them belongs entirely to us. Our truths are our own partakings and creations no matter what degree of universal validity we ascribe to them—again, as our own adherences. These, our beliefs, are we.

Without them we would lack salt, savor, spine. They are vital to our entitlement as human beings. Their sanctions do not occur in the world outside our subjectivity, but consist of our sense of their "rightness" for us, our acceptance of their validity.

We are responsible for holding our beliefs in that we agent our approving them. As adults all of us decide more or less awarely whether our past restraints and constraints of which we're cognizant deserve our continuing allegiance. We also are free, even obligated to ourselves, to weigh them and revise them as we change toward them. We alter them and in turn are re-formed by their shiftings. If we shun this prerogative, this duty to our personhood, we continue the sellout of our right to rely on our own inner promptings and resonatings in response to the input we receive from beyond our bodies. Such individual messages are the only legitimate, truly existent, sanctions for our standards, judgments and commitments.

When we acknowledge we choose our adherences, we by implication honor them as worthy of our support. Perhaps we even are willing to credit ourselves for our selecting them.

Guilt and Shame

Our own criteria cause us to feel guilt about our behaviors, shame over our very natures. The promptings of guilt are our judgments, largely suppressed from awareness, of our sellout to the world: renunciation of our wants, likes and emotions destined to invite trouble with other people; replacement of our aims for ourselves with those not our own forthcomings. Shame flagellates us for all failings in accommodating to our scenes.

To own our sellout is to experience in full our shame and guilt at its occurrence. Concomittantly we yearn for our original selves often seemingly lost forever.

Corollaries

Our adaptive guilt internalizes and reflects society's somewhat unacknowledged supposition: Rights of others are antecedent to one's own. Concurrence may serve as coin for seeking to purchase exemption from external retribution.

Addiction of any type narcotizes the conflict between our authentic and adaptive selves.

By labelling others we attempt to shame them into behaviors that accord with our shoulds or desires for them. Even if our parenthood of them is actual, not solely functional, we well may choose correcting them to disguise for us emotions of our own which we criticize as childlike.

We bully with criticism to improve our self-image. As victimizers, we feel smarter, more righteous and powerful, than those whom we subjugate. We may cultivate reactions of guilt as proof of our decency. Resenting the psychic discomfort such pangs cause us, we work to lessen their effect with conclusions such as, "She asked for it." To prove the point and justify our belittling behavior, we continue it.

Internalization

Probable attempts by us, presumably unconscious and begun in childhood, to become praiseworthy to our parents or their surrogates breed our introjections of—identifications with—our images of those persons. Chances are strong these processes increased our likenesses to our models, and perhaps also our consequent opportunities of proving more pleasing to them.

Our internal versions were and are more controllable than the people external to ourselves which they reflect. Within us, placating efforts are constantly workable. Unfortunately, as outward successes elude, inner self-criticisms in chase of them increase. Avoiding them could breed the rebelliousness which proclaims "I chose and choose to be different from you. So there!"

Repetition Compulsion

A drive to counteract the sense of helplessness from which we may suffer could explain readily the "repetition compulsion." We can consider this term designates at least in part our unconscious attempt to reproduce in some subsequent relationship our experience with a parent, usually of the sex opposite from our own.

When we feel incompetent we protect ourselves from the need to cope with new happening. The message we send ourselves runs somewhat thus: "I don't behave in an adequate way. I seem to use the wrong tools. I've got to discover the right ones by mastering this situation. If I move on first, I'll only botch my other chances."

We must choose persons similar to the parents whom we feel we failed to satisfy. Otherwise, our successes elsewhere can't persuade us that we either have learned whatever lessons we overlooked, or that fault lay not with us but with, instead, our judges. Which way we estimate outcome depends, probably, on our temperaments. Do we orient ourselves toward controlling others by means of becoming effective? Or do we more strongly wish to believe we can please them? We then would long to trust in our original innocence.

We can redeem our sellout.

5. RECLAMATION

As children we feared that without our self-abandonment, be it marginal or pervasive, we could not survive. Our choices centered not on whether we sacrificed a portion of our autonomy, but how.

In first comprehending fully our early situation, most of us rage at others and ourselves, and grieve, over sacrifices of our innerness. Eventually we realize we deserve our own forgiveness for our self-disownings. We now understand they occurred because they appeared to us, often accurately, as fully necessary to continuing our existence. Freshly or anew, we recognize that as adults we need no longer depend predominantly on others for our sustenance and protection.

Apart from specifics of our individual accommodations to pressures, our method of self-sale was this: We relinquished to the world outside us at least some measure of custody over our self-awareness and choices. Our guilt and shame over betrayal of our inner lives persist until we reclaim as basis for our choices our own thoughts, feelings, desires.

We honor them through fulfilling two conditions:

(1) We need to accept that, each moment we live, we select consciously or defaultingly not only our every response to stimuli, but also each of our behaviors.

(2) We must recognize the utter subjectivity of all our beliefs, standards, criteria, allegiances, emotions, ideas, choices. It is we who agent them. Although we may think they originate elsewhere, we scarcely can deny that acceptance of their validity is our own.

Standardizing

We continually cast our votes. We also select, even draw up, the ballots we use. We are free to construct them however we please, with any degree of intensity which appeals to, or expresses, us.

Persons maintaining that God is the sanction for their credos choose, as do all of us, their every conviction, even this: Verities and moral laws not only exist in themselves, but also reach us direct from a deity. I contend that religious faith in itself is volitional. For this reason alone it can mold and depict its adherents.

Some of us tend to universalize and objectify standards. To question the independent existence of any is to legitimize challenging all, a prospect perhaps unsettling. And equating our truths with beliefs bucks much of religious teaching.

Frequently we attribute to our criteria an intrinsic, impersonal validity. Mistakenly we conceive such sanction thus: as external to the totality of all persons' individual philosophies held both awarely and unawarely. Faith we may sustain in the immanence of rightness allows us this surmise: We can possess whatever knowledge we require for controlling our compatibility with our environment, circumventing our actual or potential helplessness within it.

Attempting to counteract our powerlessness by deifying standards, we stumble into a trap. We become impotent pawns of unyielding oughts and musts. The more strongly we feel choiceless in selecting our premises and criteria, the more firmly we first adopted, as a seeming necessity of survival, whatever criteria dictate our decidings.

Questioning and Answering

In what mode or manifestation do criteria, ideas, contain autonomous validity? Its essence is what? Its substance? It locates where? In standards or criteria themselves? Within which of their aspects? As a characteristic or property of theirs?

Our truths lack essence, substance, of their own. Their authenticity derives solely from human decisions: second standards affirming the first. Measurings are no more nor less than concepts of persons. They matter not to or in themselves, but, if at all, only to measurers.

Standards aren't independent of, but are, beliefs. These, for their part, aren't separate from humans; they lack other existence. Our mental activities supply their sole substance.

Standards, criteria, validations, beliefs, all are only what-is.

And what isn't some kind of what-is—isn't.

Subjectifying

This vein of thinking liberates us to seek sanctions exclusively in our own subjectivity: those choices we base on what we are and wish for. The process invites us to reexamine our judgments. It implies our assessments can prove more inclusive than we'd realized. It assigns us charge of our being. Our autonomy itself is none other than this awareness and honoring of our innerness.

By comprehending that our reactions are conditionings, we can reach different responses. We empower ourselves to weigh, then favor or reject, for ourselves. Paradoxically, by accepting we lack the freedom not to be affected by the worlds we live in, our freedom is born.

And the more we contain the area of criteria we consider are valid in themselves, the less we constrict that freedom. So we discover that the true antidote to helplessness is our interiority.

Choosing

We trust our innerness even more strongly when we understand we cannot control our external scene. In expecting or trying to, we place ourselves at its mercy. Yet we always impact it. To do so efficiently requires we focus upon selecting among alternative possibilities for our own behaviors. Only this process equates with and gives us our power.

Not choosing is an impossibility, the one freedom we lack. Our inner fibre grows from our sense that we do indeed choose. The deeper this awareness, the sturdier our strength.

We function through our decisions, conscious and subliminal. Choice by default is impotent; by deliberate volition, potent.

We create our options only by our acts of adopting them. Until we approve them we reject them. They lie dormant, potentials only.

When we bypass active choosings to keep open all possibilities, we hand over our present, as a burnt offering, to our future.

If our choices require no external justifications, we can afford to acknowledge them as solely who we are. We concede the fact that responsibilty for our affirming them rests entirely on our shoulders. We then become invulnerable to the insistence of others and ourselves that we "ought to" switch allegiances.

Transcending

Self-reclamation lies in a realm of living nonjudgmental in that we view our evaluations as mere manifestations of ourselves. To reach it is to emerge from sellout into rebirth.

Whatever happens to us is who we are. We've the right to all of it, and to honor it. We're justified in holding within ourselves and, if we wish, sharing with others whatever "truths" we wish to confirm. Acknowledging them as our own absolves us of any requirement that we supply for them some external validation.

Only embracing our standards and credos as we, not as independently existent "facts" of the world, revocalizes those inner voices we silenced long ago.

The question becomes: Is our continuing existence still subjectively inseparable from our original convictions now perhaps tyrannical? Can we change a "yes" reply to "no"?

6. BELIEF EXTENSIONS

Earlier I postulated primary categories of Basic Beliefs (BB's) and Basic Questions (BQ's) that in my view concern the nature of the world/cosmos. I now stipulate a trio of categories, "secondaries," which refer to human modes of living in the world. They offer an array of ways in which persons can function, presenting these as philosophies of effectiveness. The final grouping I term "tertiaries." These offer a spectrum of self-imagings.

Differences among Primaries, Secondaries and Tertiaries

Phrasing a bit too broadly, I allot to the second (middle) and third (final) categories of believing these descriptions:

The secondaries showcase "what I think I ought to be"; the final set highlights "what I feel I am."

Our primary BB's condition formation of the middle three. These, in turn, affect our self-appraisals which the last threesome reflect. Learning our personal tertiaries, then secondaries, point us backward to the content of our primaries. This trio informs us of the modes of our responding, often chosen by our sellout, to the Basic Issues (BI's) with which life confronts us.

The more we uncover our own particulars of these interconnectings, the more thoroughly we can appraise our inner worlds and functionings. We then become free to alter whichever of them we wish to modify or discard.

Here I present a systemization of...

Secondary Basic Beliefs

4. The best of human judgment is: (A) absolute; or (B) contingent; or (C) relative.

5. The best of human power is: (A) controlling; or (B) nonexternalized; or (C) expressive.

6. The best of human awareness is: (A) sensating; or (B) oscillating; or (C) intuiting.

These BB's easily can be expressed as BQ's, as they are in the following chapter.

7. SECONDARY EXTENSIONS

Secondary Amplifications
4A. Is the best of human judgment absolute?
Can human judgment be based verifiably upon truths and/or standards objectively existent in themselves and universally applicable?

Are reliable touchstones for forming set beliefs available through meditation, prayer, or in sacred books?

Can reason and logic provide sure bases for constructing conclusions which are evidentially or probably correct?

4B. Is the best of human judgment contingent?
Should human judgment recognize all issues as dividable into two spheres: the subjective, in which individual determination proves appropriate; and the objective, for which applicable truths and/or standards appertain?

Ought revelation, whether provided in sacred books or through experience of the person, or should rationality indicate whether personal judgment or external guidance is in each instance the agent of choice to trust?

Can reason and logic often provide adequate bases for constructing conclusions which probably are evidentially or provably correct?

Should certainty of conviction be considered one or the only touchstone for measuring the validity of belief?

4C. Is the best of human judgment relative?
Is human judgment unable to verify any independent existence of truths and/or standards which are applicable universally?

Can every criterion for forming beliefs validate only those of and for each individual?

Is the frame of reference accurate which maintains that objectivity is illusion and subjectivity is fact?

If "there is nothing good or bad but thinking makes it so," does freedom and/or responsibility for personal opinions increase or decrease?

5A. Is the best of human power controlling?

Must all persons either dominate others or be dominated by them?

Is mastery a sign of strength, with refusing to exert it an evidence of weakness?

Should both "right makes might" and vice versa serve as guidelines for decisions and behaviors?

Is failure to take charge an irresponsibility toward self and others, inviting victimization of either or both?

Does eschewing dominance of situations and other persons breed inertia?

Is acceptance of unwelcome occurrence merely the passive resignation of the coward?

5B. Is the best of human power nonexternalized?

If "knowledge is power," by self-revelation does a person invite attack or domination?

Does expression externalize and thereby dissipate psychic energy?

Can self-containment eliminate distraction from inner discovery?

Might the most effective resistance accommodate to occurrence, rather than attempt obstruction of it?

Should the maintenance of privacy best allow inner freedom?

Is the case frequently that "familiarity breeds contempt?"

Does prudence advise "keep 'em guessing?"

5C. Is the best of human power expressive?

Might self-knowledge form through articulation?

Does objectification unclog body, mind and spirit?

Is the speaking person the one who risks, affects, and thereby is changed?

Can the energy of spontaneity promote zestful living?

Is expressiveness the nucleus of creativity?

Does revelation of belief and emotion provide the essence of intimacy?

Is the courage to specify thought and feeling persuasively authoritative?

6A. Is the best of human awareness sensating?

Does human experience base itself in the body?

Is the physical self the only real source of instinctual knowing?

Do human senses provide all knowledge that truly is individual?

Does sensory awareness of the self and the world yield the fullest sense of aliveness, and give the experience most rich and varied?

Might the philosophy of "eat, drink and be merry, for tomorrow we die" prove the most realistic?

Does the body remember it gives the human its being?

6B. Is the best of human awareness oscillating?

Is the full range of human experiencing available only through employment of all faculties?

Can sensory awareness tune in to the tangible, while intuitive divinings more strongly touch on the intangible and transpersonal?

Do sensatings move from the outer world inward, while intuitions reversly flow from within to without?

Are divinations as personal to the knower as are sensations?

6C. Is the best of human awareness intuiting?

Is the knowledge intuition yields unobtainable through any other faculty?

Can divination singly provide the true core of human experience?

Does solely the intuitive sense give personal knowledge that is real of inner and outer worlds?

For each person, is the only unerring information a divining of what seems so?

Does all truly individual knowing consist of an experiential contact with its object?

Might intuitive awareness of self and world yield the fullest, most accurate sense of realities?

Can intuition alone dissolve an illusory division between the knower and the known, uniting human being with total universe?

8. BASIC BELIEFS ABOUT OURSELVES

Previously I explain my division of basic beliefs (BB's) into three sets: primaries/secondaries/tertiaries. As a totality they concern, respectively, our sense of...

system/scene/self

Expressed in a manner less formularized, the categories of BB's cover our emotions and deductions concerning: (1) the nature of the universe;

(2) optimum human behaviors; (3) our personal characteristics.

Below I offer a system of tertiaries. I amplify it in the "Expansions of Tertiary Beliefs/Questions" which follows it immediately.

Tertiary Basic Beliefs

7. I tend to see myself as: (A) guilty; or (B) accountable; or (C) innocent.

8. I tend to see myself as: (A) ineffectual; or (B) inconsistent; or (C) accomplishing.

9. I tend to see myself as: (A) alienating; or (B) available; or (C) attracting.

9. TERTIARY EXTENSIONS

Tertiary Amplifications

7A. Do I tend to see myself as guilty?

Am I apt to assume the negatives in my life are "all my fault"?

Do I think other persons hold doubtful or low opinions of me only or mainly if I give them cause?

Do I try by harsh self-judgments to motivate my improvement?

Am I constantly measuring my thoughts, feelings and behaviors according to exacting standards?

Do I take pride in criticizing my character and performance as indicating my standards for myself are high?

Do I hope to buy off external punishments by inflicting my own as self-beratings?

Does telling myself "the fault is mine" allow me also to feel in charge of outcome?

7B. Do I tend to see myself as accountable?

Do I concede that feelings and thoughts I repress, not only those I'm aware of, affect my actions?

Do I accept that I'm responsible for my choices of behaviors?

Do I consider I produce my thoughts, beliefs, convictions, standards, emotions and deeds?

Can I admit my contributions to negative aspects of personal relationships?

Can I regret an action and learn from it without undue self-chasement?

Am I usually not subject to an excruciating sense of guilt?

Do I accept I'm in charge of only myself, not other people?

Do I view myself as half responsible, no more, for the circumstances of my life?

Do I acknowledge I don't control events, only my responses to them?

7C. Do I tend to see myself as innocent?

Do I believe free will is a myth?

Am I convinced all my deeds, and even my thoughts and feelings, fulfill a purpose prescribed by the universe?

In my view, through cosmic design does everything happen for the best?

Regardless of my actions, in my opinion is taking care of themselves solely the job of others?

Do I hold myself not in the least responsible for anyone else's reactions to my behaviors?

In my opinion, is sin simply not attempting to grow, and one I don't lay claim to?

In my estimation, if I feel guilty am I erroneously assuming that when I acted I could or should have been a different person?

Do I target insight as the one expatiation for a mistake which the universe requires?

Is changing the only penance I think I owe the world for any wrongdoing of mine?

8A. Do I tend to see myself as ineffectual?

Do I often feel the level of my intelligence is not very high?

Do I judge I'm slow to learn?

Do I consider I lack special skills, abilities or talents?

Do I view my training and education as permanently disadvantaged?

Am I seemingly unable to choose and pursue a life's course?

Do I basically lack ambition?

Do I consider one or more professions would intrigue me more were I by nature not somewhat inadequate for all?

In my opinion, do I lack enthusiasms because my abilities to pursue my potential interests are suspect?

Am I a follower, not a leader?

Am I usually anxious about the judgments others will levy against my performances?

If appraisals of me are negative, do I feel I therefore deserve them?

Do I wonder if others sense my self-doubt and decide if it's present it's justified?

Am I suspicious that my insecurities prove by existing that they're realistic?

Do I or would I judge mere good luck to be the cause of fortuitous happening in my life?

Do I theorize I at least avoid disappointments if I don't expect too much of myself?

8B. Do I tend to see myself as inconsistent?

Do I feel my level of intelligence is fairly high in some fields but somewhat low in others?

Do I consider my interest, regardless of its intensity, to be no measure of my aptitude?

Can I manage to console myself that my gifts outweigh and justify my insufficiencies?

Am I inclined to accept the judgments, for better or for worse, which people pass on my performances as more realistic than my own?

Do I often feel anxious about how I did or will acquit myself in the eyes of others?

Am I too frequently the butt of harsh self-criticisms?

Do I find my modesty in appraising myself rather gratifying?

Am I afraid self-pride might go before a fall?

8C. Do I tend to see myself as accomplishing?

Do I rate my intelligence as superior?

Do I judge that I evidence at least one talent or skill to an outstanding degree?

Do I effectively use my abilities?

Am I satisfied with my to-date achievements?

Am I as knowledgeable as I need to be for succeeding in the ways I wish?

Do I try to be aware of options open to me?

Are my choices deliberate, not accidental?

Am I purposefully directive of my plans and actions in pursuit of an ambition or goal?

Can I clearly state to myself what I wish to acomplish in the future?

Do I work and play energetically?

Do the judgments of others pertaining to me matter to me only slightly, if at all?

Do I consider the independence of my self-appraisals gives evidence of their validity?

Do I view my opinions and judgments as generally more trustworthy than those of other persons?

To me, is undeserved modesty not a virtue?

Is self-confidence to my mind the product of merit?

9A. Do I tend to see myself as alienating?

Do I often appear to rub people the wrong way?

Am I sometimes accused outright of behaving in an overbearing or bossy manner?

Do others often arouse my impatience?

Do I judge the majority of conversations among people to be trivial?

Do I find difficulty in making friends?

Are my communications with others frequently misunderstood by them?

Am I plagued by feelings of loneliness?

Do I suffer the sense that no one truly knows the person I am?

In my opinion, does self-revelation tend to invite rejection?

Is it true that the more independent of people I am, the stronger I feel?

Am I glad I don't allow others to walk over me?

9B. Do I tend to see myself as available?

Do I view myself as friendly, though not clinging, with others?

Do I like many persons, but by no means all?

Do I consider my appraisals of people to be realistic yet not harsh?

Do I often enjoy the company of acquaintances and friends?

Can I relish not only conviviality but also solitude?

Can I accept at times arousing negative reactions in others without undergoing more than a temporary loss of self-esteem?

Do I consider my self-appraisals as valid as opinions others might hold of me?

In my view, do I communicate understandably with people?

Do I feel at least a few other persons know me fairly well?

Do I not fear rejection to a handicapping degree?

Overall, do my relationships with others appear to illustrate a "middle way"?

9C. Do I tend to see myself as attracting?

Do I consider one of my major strongpoints is my ability to get along with people?

Am I an understanding, sympathetic listener?

Can I readily put myself in another person's shoes?

According to my philosophy, does some good reside in nearly everyone, if not in all?

Do I think most harm results from persons' ignorance, rather than their unkindness?

Do I judge myself not too harshly?

Is my credo never to hurt another's sensitivities more than absolutely necessary?

Am I inclined to feel I've failed whoever doesn't like me?

Do I not allow myself behavior I view as rejecting?

Is it my view that relationships are the source of the happiness that's deepest?

Do I sometimes feel lonesome, but seldom lonely?

Do I consider true loners are somewhat unsuccessful human beings?

10. FURTHER OBSERVATIONS

Comments

I wish, somewhat whimsically, to suggest that, generally speaking, persons belong in either of two camps, as those who...

...(1) are willing to feel guilty so they can feel also in control; or

...(2) are willing to feel out of control so they also can feel innocent.

I recommend this aim in living: enhancement of awareness to extend the areas of conscious choices..

Emotions

Only our self-knowledge which is experiential, not merely ideological, can cure us of our inner renunciations. The agent of rediscovery is our emotion, felt in full, rather than mainly examined for cause. And how we relive and treat our feelings depends on our views of them. Do they, or some of them, frighten us? We then at such times can remind ourselves that only our choices determine our behaviors.

Our feelings reveal our true attitudes toward any and every subject, provided we don't use attitudes to deny these feelings. Until we're willing to own them, we of course can block our acknowledgment of their presence. We're then able to manufacture, for perceived reasons of safety or morality, emotions seemingly more appropriate. Our beliefs, basic or auxiliary, conduct the process. Needed for coverup, they remain or become unavailable to our reappraisal.

Subjectivity

Our entertaining a thought or feeling offers no guarantee of its appropriateness or interpretive accuracy. We merely are manifesting an aspect of our being, one which, like all such others we hold, is a candidate for re-evalutaion. Any reassessing it, too, is simply another facet of our individual personhood. All our ideas and emotions are representations of solely our own interiors. If we conceive them to be externally inspired, the affirmation of them is our own.

We might label "scene" the objectivity, and "self" the subjectivity, with "system" designated the substratum of both. But the scene is always also our own experience. So all is subjectivity, externally to us neither right nor wrong. Objectivity is illusion. We consequently are free and entitled to live our innerness as we please. This assertion is foundational.

Subject/Object Split

For inward examination we often dissect ourselves into subject and "its" appraised focal points: current responses, even our traits. That in ourselves which we evaluate we in the process attempt to objectify. In illusory fashion our appraising mode functions as subject. Into its object it consigns all else pertaining to us.

Identifying with our judging, we fallaciously perceive its foci to be existent beyond our self-boundaries. We register our reactions as externalized, rather than as occurring within. Because they seem to lie outside of us, we can't truly feel them to be the who we in the moment are.

Often we thereby advantageously gain new views of ourselves. But we also at least to some extent disown our direct experience of that innerness we elect to scrutinize. We can really claim as ourselves only those interior happenings we embrace as our burgeoning of the present. Until we do so we're unable to recognize these occurrences as the actual "whats" which are our "I."

Self-Appraisal

If we don't question the sanction and standards of our appraiser, don't view its voice as the product of conditioning, our choices can't be free. They become determined by our evaluator's unchallenged criteria. Yet autonomy consists of our unfettered capacity to select consciously and knowledgeably from among possibilities of belief and consequent behavior.

Aspects of ourselves we criticize, then disown, don't dissolve and evaporate. They control us beyond our awareness, pulling our strings from the rear and pit of our psyches. They join with our unexamined dicti in robbing us of our liberty to choose and act responsibly. We can't listen openly to, and learn from, messages offered us by our sides which we stifle with disapproval.

The self-flagelation our appraiser often lays on us causes us basic, complex and ever-widening unhappiness: We become unable to like who we are.

Deep within, we yearn to experience ourselves as wholes, unitings of multiple facets. Our subject/object split frustrates this human longing. We are wise to examine the inner harmfulness of dividing our consciousness. We could opt for allowing ourselves to be merely self-aware.

Psychic Unity

For me, the goal of inner work is sensing ourselves increasingly often to be subjects only. The occurrence persuades us of the psychic unity we crave. Conflicts appear as often-transitory formings within it, rather than as warring and segregated complexes which endure.

We consist of a multitude of capacities, potentialities. In any moment these can fulfill themselves, as processes within us, only partially. We host no collection of active and dormant entities, omnipresent subselves.

Healing

Our admonitions and rules invade the natural process of our psychic growth and even block its movement. But unimpeded, the curative power residing within us humans is to me awesome.

Simply to experience our subjectivity is to redeem our sellout. The process requires our eliminating nothing. We can deal with troublesome aspects of ourselves by recognizing we're also those they differ from. Both kinds of characteristic are there in us; most of us scarcely glimpse the scope of our own complexities. Acknowledging our counterbalances changes us organically, from within.

All sides of us speak in part through our Basic Beliefs.

11. SPOTLIGHTING THEORY

Introduction

Material which follows adapts a theory and method titled Voice Dialogue. It was devised by Stone and Winkelman/Stone.

I term procedures I propose "spotlighting" because they differ too much from Voice Dialogue to pass as its near-duplicate. In describing my approach, if I retain the label the Stones adopt I to some degree would misrepresent their system. Whenever possible I forego the use of their terminology. Nowhere am I attempting to imply a comment on their work. Nor do I think negatively in any way of their perspectives; my variations merely fit better for me.

Perspective

I image personality as one human world. That of everyone consists of energy conditioned, hence individualized, both potential and kinetic, forming and functioning in particular modes. These constitute our subselves, sides. An evoker—therapist, friend or the explorer singly—invites particular facets of personality (I term them "subselves" or "sides"), one by one to express themselves.

We all entertain viewpoints and feelings which differ and even conflict among themselves. An increase in our knowledge of these various manifestations within our totalness works its own organic change in us. We need do no more than truly notice and accept our multiplicities. Paradoxically, attending to them lessens their hidden strength; they can stop their unrecognized efforts to gain our awareness of them.

I elect to invest in fostering the experience of the psyche as a unity in continual change, and capable always of becoming more vast. All of us can expand ourselves as our experience widens, provided we allow it to become more conscious.

I think of psychic growth as a process of ever-increasing inclusions into awareness of all our human aspects. I advocate no exclusions, nor any sensing and concept of permanent partitionment within us. I consider one outcome of successful inner work is the dissolution of every interior set, but artificial, demarcation we persons conceive.

The Fluid Self

People, like all else, are energies which, not being essences, interact. Personality contains no permanent or impermeable boundaries. Neither total self nor subself exists as a persisting entity, ready to become apparent. Inner divisions occur as fluidities; aspects of psyche flow one into the other.

Total self is potential only which in any one moment is partly kinetic.

Our subselves—or, to term them differently, the facets of our personhood—aren't structural, but functional and, when we work with them, methodological. They're our possibilities activated, actualized, by circumstances.

All of our personality sides, like the thoughts and feelings which manifest them, are inventions and creations of our living present. Their source is our full potential, with most of it lying dormant in every instant. From this vast reservoir that each of us consists of, we extract a few aspects, always temporarily.

Subselves aren't constant. They fade in and out of appearance and effectiveness. They rise up, to disappear into the ocean of our conditioned and individualized capacities. They sleep and then revive. They die and resurrect.

Personality sides aren't partitionings of self. Rather, they occur as tendencies, not structures, active or passive momentarily. They incline toward manifesting cohesively in circumstances appropriate to them. In whole, they constitute the "self" of our "system/scene/self." External happenings provide our scene.

Conflicts can exist among subselves. At times our thoughts oppose one another; some of our feelings contradict other emotions; and intents grapple with their opposites we also host. Compatibilities among all combine, creating transitorily one of our subselves. Their operation as a unit lies dormant until a pertinent situation evokes them jointly.

Spotlighting can serve as a magnet drawing forth our subselves, archetypal and individualized.

Nature of Awareness

Like blood coursing through our bodies, our subself, Awareness, permeates our psyches. It occurs in two modes: detached and identifying. Their energies differ. When Awareness includes a sense of encompassing that which it watches, it has identified, expanded. Objects of its observations appear to occur inside itself.

If the focus of Awareness seems separate from and outside its own energy, it has detached, contracted. It thereby creates a sense of subject/object split which actually is artificial. If we truly aren't divided from all else, neither is our Awareness.

Through recognizing itself as a portion of the contents of our consciousness, Awareness can identify with them, each and all. It then perceives them as the aspects of a totality to which it, too, belongs.

We might consider our Awareness centers in or as the space, the void, which separates conflicting claims subselves exert. Arising midway between their polar extremities, at its widest it can embrace them both. Awareness, being energy, takes many forms: with various people and with the same person at different times.

Aware Chooser

Our directiveness continually connects and merges with our Awareness. I term the resulting energy—this ubiquitous subself—our Aware Chooser.

Living seems impelled by two forces: one effecting unification; the other, individuation. Within the microcosm of each of us, Awareness fosters unifying; choosing, through its discriminations, promotes individualizing. The wider our Awareness, the larger is the area of self our choices can involve. Limitations on our Awareness are those our Choosers set.

Our Chooser, too, appears at zero point on a spectrum. Its continuum is that of intent. The inner process of selection and willing occurs constantly. Our receptor subselves, potentialities when dormant, become kinetic when our Aware Chooser activates them, giving them a green light to "go ahead." The Chooser's mode of energizing a side, like that which our Awareness employs, is identification with it.

But our Awareness can register firmly this actuality concerning any subself: It occurs as only one among many. Expressed in different words: "This side, too, is I, yet unquestionably not all of me."

Thus informed, our Chooser energy then begins to experience itself no longer as if it were one of our other sides, or several of them. Cognizant as Aware Chooser of its distinctiveness from the rest, it can exert its true function and serve as referee, choice-maker, among their conflicting claims. Merely by this determining whether and when it will allow particular energies to act, our Aware Chooser separates from them sufficiently for its decision-making.

Existing within the inclusiveness of Awareness as ground of our choosing, polarities our subselves create in our psyches lose their divisiveness. They now seem to occur along an expanding spectrum. As points on a continuum, even slight variations can highlight themselves.

Notice of thoughts and feelings that differ however subtly can supply us with a reminder: All our manifestations of innerness are matched by others contrasting with them. This recognition liberates our sides for their natural balancing of one another. I view each as a portion of our wholes.

Acceptance of Subselves

When we realize the purpose—our protection—a dominant subself attempts to serve, we no longer need feel ashamed of it. A victim side, for example, allows us to circumvent feeling guilty for our errors of judgment.

In reliving our sellout, we acknowledge that our survival demanded development of personality aspects we now may find troublesome. Our issue then becomes one of reassessment. Is a belief and its emotional syndrome functionally constructive in the present? Or would we benefit from its modification attained by permitting opposite facets of ourselves to thrive also?

In Spotlighting work, we call out subselves in sequence for our specific purposes of acquaintance, then reappraisal, and always temporarily. When a communication with one of our sides is finished, it fades once more from foreground into background.

We next begin exploration of conscious connection with sides of the psyche.

12. SPOTLIGHTING METHOD

Overview

We can practice Spotlighting either alone or, perhaps preferably, with assistance from a helper. In either case, techniques remain the same.

The Evoker, whether she or he be only ourselves or a co-worker, directly talks with and questions sides—facets, aspects—of our Explorer selves (I term them "Searchers"). The subpersonality expressed, in being afforded its own autonomy, is thus temporarily separated from all else comprising our personhood—i.e., detached from the whole of our psyches—and given complete attention. As fully as possible the self-examiner identifies with the expressed sub-person, sub-psyche. To her, it accordingly becomes "I, the side." The person in totality refers to herself as "I, the self." Either side or self can be assigned or use the Searcher's name, along with these appropriate, descriptive designations.

Evokers present the spectrum of belief options. We spotlight in sequence those subselves our Choosers elect and allow to appear.

The Evoker eschews judgments or any assist with decidings, for these belong in the province of only the Searcher's Chooser.

Advantages of Spotlighting

Assets of Spotlighting appear to be that it:

> 1. decontaminates our reactions from those in us that differ;
>
> 2. allows us to experience specific thoughts and feelings subjectively;
>
> 3. divulges our incompatibilities and conflicts.

Disadvantages of Spotlighting

Drawbacks of Spotlighting appear to be that it:

> 1. implies our psyches consist of more or less permanent partitions;

2. seems to treat our subselves as objects to our subject Aware Choosers;

3. seems to treat our total selves as objects to our subselves;

4. impedes intermingling of contrasting thoughts and feelings which an issue may involve.

Subselves as Hosts of Beliefs

Work with our subselves ("parts," "personality parts") must remain purely evocative, of their beliefs also. No helper should instruct, or require a side, or part, to judge itself, its statements, opinions or commitments. Reevalutations should occur only between Evokers and Aware Choosers. When personality sides feel themselves called to account, they withdraw and shut down.

Each of our Basic Beliefs (BB's) can be viewed as a dynamic of a subself. Through expressing belief as belonging to its appropriate side, a self-investigator can gain an actual feel for the functioning of that belief—its cause, continuing purpose, method and style of operation—as a vital aspect of him or her in whole. I wish to encourage Evokers in learning about it as fully as possible through its self-revelation: its history, function and goals in behalf of their totalities.

We can find a somewhat general name for our side who thinks or feels in accordance with a BB, then converse with it as holder, rather than as exemplification, of the premise under examination.

Put somewhat differently, we Evokers are wise to eschew addressing a belief directly, as if it constitutes a subself. Instead, we can talk with a more comprehensive side, its name to be drawn from a Searcher's input, about its motivating premises. When we question the part we substitute "your belief" for "you." This procedure allows the voicing subself to disassociate, if it wishes, from the pertinent premise.

To give an example: Investigation could begin with a side who postulates that commitment to any marriage always should be upheld, regardless of circumstances. This subself could be designated the moralist, say, who affirms this belief among others. The part then can be asked to weigh whether it might not retain its sense of morality even though it modifies the particular conviction, might not find a different criterion for an ethics less constrictive.

Specifically, I propose that we don't ask a Searcher if we might speak "...with your belief that...," but rather, "...with the side of you who believes...

The greater our awareness of conflicting beliefs, the more able we are to recognize that none of these alone, without its opposite, can represent our total selves. For just as we in whole consist of complex and unharmonious facets, so do our convictions clash, perhaps within but surely among, our subselves. They become able to select alternatives offered by any and, at least in theory, every inner persuasion, drawing in all possibilities appropriate to the moment.

To summarize: BB's serve better purpose as Basic Questions (BQ's) to ask our subselves, not as those sides themselves. Put differently, subselves should be considered more comprehensive than, but inclusive of, BB's, yet not merely synonymous with, or identical to, them.

Relevant Considerations

Although in Spotlighting practice we connect with sides sequentially, in actuality they can function simultaneously.

To question spotlighted energies about other occurrings within the personality—about, say, its friends and enemies within the whole of the psyche—is possibly to turn the side into subject and all else within the person into object. We're best advised to stay within and with the subjectivity of the Explorer's side until we return to the individual's whole.

We might wish to ascertain which BB's impinge upon a specific problem under investigation. We could ask to speak with the philosopher subself who decides the nature of life, interprets events. This side in all probability feeds its conclusions, impressions, sensings about The Way Matters Stand to the Chooser.

Subselves

Names ascribable to the sides we contact are generally those of traits we possess or roles we play in life. Descriptive phrases sometimes can prove the most relevant, because the most individualized, of all designations.

Subselves (personality parts) seem to divide somewhat readily into four categories: powerful, mediating, instinctual, and childlike. Examples of each grouping are:

Powerful

appraising, evaluating, rational, impersonal, dispassionate, comparing, critical, judgmental, perfectionist, omnipotent, fundamentalist, patriarchal, punitively parental, guilty, victimized, responsible, ambitious, achieving, competitive, combative, cruel, murderous, dishonest, deceptive, etc.

Mediating

These sides concern themselves primarily with interpersonal relationships. Some of them are: supportively parental, pleasing, placating, unperturbed, instructive, explanatory, tolerant, understanding, understandable, compassionate, forgiving, commending, gentle, kind, etc.

Instinctual

angry, envious, jealous, selfish, aggressive, lazy, relaxed, fun-loving, adventurous, untraditional, free-spirited, enthusiastic, sensual, flirtatious, sexual, self-accepting, loving, creative, spiritual, etc.

Childlike

open, vulnerable, trusting, receptive, spontaneous, eager, joyful, playful, daydreaming, imaginative, inventive, intuitive, sensitive, self-protective, anxious, fearful, needy, etc.

Many attributes listed as typical of specific subself groups clearly apply also to others.

We access our sellout through contact with our open child, a designation referring to all of our youthful subselves. When none of these is promptly accessible to us, the Evoker can spotlight an intermediary side. This part can describe the child and the enforced compromises she or he endured.

The Appraiser

This ubiquitous side functions as, or through, many of our powerful subselves. Its spirit is closest to that of our critic. Aligning with our evaluator, moralist, fundamentalist, matriarch and patriarch, it also feeds its judgments to our pushers and protectors.

The Appraiser pays little attention to our uniqueness. Its goal is our conformity to standards of what and how we ought to be and act. Its concern is the scale or criterion of measurement, not our individuality.

When we're in the appraising mode we objectify all of ourselves we're evaluating. This energy lacks interest in exploring and understanding what for us actually is. It focuses solely on what it thinks ought to be. Self-appraisal is one of our psyche's main devices of escape from subjectivity into self-objectification.

When we forsake our innerness, our question becomes "How will I be perceived by others?" rather than "How do I wish to act?" We focus on "What should I do?" instead of asking "What is it I want to do?" We examine the issue of "Why am I like I am?", overlooking "How do I feel about who I am?"

I brand tyranical criteria as a main source of psychological distress. One method we can use to modify, at least, the force of our Appraiser is to insist it identify its sanctions.

13. COMMUNICATING WITH SUBSELVES

Spotlighting Beliefs

For initiating Spotlighting work with Basic Beliefs (BB's), Evokers can use these or similar remarks:

"I seem to encounter a side of you who believes...I'd like to learn more about this you. So I ask that when we work with this subself's believing you try to sense and feel merely that single side of you, to identify with only this partial you as fully as possible. For this period, if you're willing, you'll talk, feel and think as if your subself who holds this belief—or maybe some other conviction, too—were the only you who exists. You'll voice just the thoughts and feelings of this one side. You'll give this partial you full rein for expression. During that time you'll ignore all other aspects of yourself, leaving out any which conflict. Afterward we'll talk with the whole of you again.

"You, the full person, we'll call 'self'. We'll consider your subself your 'side'. If you wish, you can find a fitting place for this partial you, an area or seat the whole of you isn't occupying. Then you'll take a minute to become the facet of you who entertains the belief itself as it lives in you."

In the conduct of a typical Spotlighting session the Evoker might ask: "May I talk with you, the frightened child?" or "...with your fear?" Or "...with the side of you who feels afraid?" With equal appropriateness s/he could state: "I wish to speak with the aspect of you who believes..." All involved could learn thereby the flavor of a credo, as well as its mode of operation, within the individual.

Our personality sides invariably are broader than the convictions they hold. One method of ascertaining the wider nature of these container subpsyches is to ask ourselves, "Who or what in me would hold this belief? What purposes would it serve for which aspects of me?"

Principal questions we might put to the selected subself are these:

    1. What vulnerability does your belief protect?

    2. What vulnerability does your belief allow?

Alternatively, a Searcher might find more immediately comprehensible the wording which follows:

    1. From what does your belief protect your full (total) self?

    2. What risks, if any, does your belief allow your whole (total) self to run?

Some or all of these questions below Evokers can ask the Searcher's subself adhering to each belief we decide to explore. They merely are samples to use or ignore. We naturally are free to employ any other queries which occur to us.

The first set of inquiries is designed to elicit the flavor of this believing side, this genuine and whole subself who holds a history, and who lives sensations, emotions and thoughts.

Some of the questions we can ask subselves are grouped below. The few preceded by an asterik are assigned twice—i.e., beneath two headings We can reword the initial inquiries for use with a childlike side.

To Ask Any Side (Subself, Part)

What are you feeling right now?

When did you first come into being?

How do your parents, living or dead, affect you?

Is there any emotion which is predominantly characteristic of you?

In what ways do you as side communicate with your full self?

What is your full self's past/present attitude toward you as side?

Would you like to change the current attitude of your whole self toward you, the side? If yes, what would you have it become?

Does your full self pay as much attention to you as you'd like?

What do you want from your whole (total) self (that you're now not getting)?

What other parts of your total self are allies of you, the subself?

What sides of your full personhood work against your best interests as a subself?

Are you growing stronger or weaker?

In what ways, if any, do you wish your full self were different or would change?

In what ways, if any, would you as a subself care to change?

What advice can you, the side, offer the whole (full self) of you?

What is your major philosophy, your code, that characterizes you, the side?

Does your total self agree in the main with your philosophy as side?

What other beliefs does this you speaking now promote?

What beliefs does your full self hold that you disagree with? Do you try to undermine them?

To Ask Any but a Childlike Side

Are you male or female?

In what ways have you changed since you first came into being?

Would you prefer, as side, to be fully in charge of the life of your total self?

If you were, in fact, in charge, would you handle matters differently? If so, in what way(s)?

Can you describe your body when (if ever) you take charge of it?

What is your opinion of your body?

How do you affect your body?

On the whole, do you like the total person you're a portion of?

To Ask Powerful Sides

*How do you help your total person?

Are there ways in which you think you're a detriment to your full self?

Do you consider that on the whole you help or hinder your whole self?

To Ask Mediating Sides

*How do you help your total person?

Which do you feel more strongly, frustrated or useful?

To Ask Instinctual Sides

*What angers you most?

What is your usual mood?

To Ask Childlike Sides

What frightens you most?

What hurts you most?

*What angers you most?

When are you happiest?

Socratic Questioning

At times Explorers might decline to express personality sides. We then can employ a Socratic type of questioning. This method, as may be apparent, seeks to imply or query, "Why is your answer the actual case?" It is one which can initiate an interior challenge of assumptions and shoulds. Evokers can gently lead on until Explorers, for themselves, conclude: Inner freedom comes with recognizing that oughts are subjectivities.

Further Suggestions for Self-Exploration

In summary, I propose that we:

1. Delve as deeply as we can into our emotions or moods, registering their physical impacts and, should they occur, analogous imageries.

2. When we feel overrun by one of our sides, turn our attention to another whose perspective provides a contrast;

3. And/or summon our Awareness.

4. Before beckoning to our Chooser, listen to as many other subselves as seem appropriate to our current issue.

I reiterate my continual hope: May all of us become convinced we consciously can choose whether or not we'll adopt and commit to what criteria, since all are forever and only innerness.

14. IN CONCLUSION

An Alternative Approach

The search for self-knowledge is to me more productive when it concerns what-is, not why.

Some persons may prefer not to examine their belief systems. They also might feel reluctant to employ Spotlighting. They could wish merely to talk of current issues in their lives. What then?

After they accept an invitation to describe their concerns, a helper (or they themselves) might respond with this observation: "Here's what I'm hearing. Does it match your actual experience?" And: "Do you consider your options include...?"

Enough from any outside agent.

My Perspective

I'm infected with my own agnosticism. The premise from which I now operate both internally and externally is this: I can't really divine another person's interior processes. In my view, neither can s/he be sure of them. I fully believe we're all essentially unknowable to everyone including ourselves.

I can entertain and even articulate whatever opinions I please including those pertaining to other people. But I want to offer all my observations—any time, anywhere—as expressions of possibilities, not facts. I wish to relinquish all necessity to theorize about anyone's motivations. Or else I deny the right of each individual to function as his or her own self-analyst. No one else understands us more fully than do we ourselves because only we can live our interiority. An attitude of "I know you better than you know yourself" invades the privacy and autonomy of its target. It also belittles the essential mystery of each human being. I'd rather honor one and all as not only unique but also ineffable and miraculous.

If we bypass all other methods of inner search, our main tool of self-discovery, I've come to conclude, can be exploring a question we or a helper can ask of ourselves. It is this: "What are my body's sensations, my thoughts and feelings, especially those of this moment?"

I don't intend this attitude as a comment on any therapeutic practitioner. I'm aware that other perspectives on the profession are just as valid as mine. In any and every discipline, varieties of thought and action offer enrichments we need. For all of us mortals belong to one perishable and cherishable world.

V

CONFESSIONS OF MY MARITAL SELF

1. AN EXCERPT

[Adapted from my book, *Vortex: A Personal Quest into the Nature of What Is*, published by prism press in 1981]:

Love: the very quickening, the beat and flow, self-granted, of all being and becoming.

Love, even when functioning as fury, is neither more nor less than life's most basic affirmation of itself.

Love is pure fact, a moment's dance of joy. To evoke it is to receive a gift from life.

Your mere relating with me is a bonus to me of existing. For me, all your feelings as they touch on our connecting are gratuitous and kingly because out of my control. I'm their focal point only.

Should you not feel affection for me you're just as unloving toward me as I'm unattracting of you. You as much as I agent negatives between us.

If I appeal to you I'm lucky. If I don't, I lose but am not shamed. I'm neither undeserving nor deserving of devotion from you.

Half the difficulty relatings cause us is that we infer an import from them, hence value them other than for per se delights and disappointments. We also insist love provide our living a patterning to rely on. So we demand of our feelings and those of others that they endure.

To whom or what do I insist that I should never suffer loss? To life? What else am I? All claims are then disguised demands on myself, bars with which I confine and imprison no person or force not me.

2. A LETTER

Dearest Adam,

I'm writing this letter because I don't want to harangue you with verbiage when you first come home.

After telling me you'd call as soon as your plane touched ground, you failed to phone from the airport. I suspect you didn't care to keep your business buddy waiting. Anyway, you left me worrying for three hours about whether or not you were safely in California. Anxiously I called the hotel where you two were registered. Apparently my message was given to you as soon as you arrived and you felt henpecked in front of Eric. So, tucked away in your own room, you phoned with the announcement that you weren't my "puppet." I expressed my own anger and hung up. Then I called you back for our fairly long talk.

Your claiming innocence with "I hadn't realized you'd be so upset at not hearing from me" I found maddening. By implying I hadn't made myself clear you dumped your burden on me. Yet we'd discussed and agreed about our contacts when you're gone. Why the hell couldn't you say, "I was inconsiderate and I apologize"?

All you needed to tell me was, in effect, this: "I don't love you very much right now; I'm too angry. But when I'm not, I do love you." Yet your attitude was, "I shouldn't have to reassure you when I'm mad." I think your reaction was rigid.

From now on when you travel forget calling. Just continue to give me your trip statistics. I'll phone the airlines myself.

You claim you want me to care about you. So when you blow it and are inconsiderate and hurt me, there'll be angry feelings. If you punish me for them as severely as you did last night by withholding all expressions of warmth, you put a premium on my own withdrawal. And you didn't seem sad that we were at odds, though you claimed you were. After I cried out, "Adam, don't do this!" you did come closer, it's true. But you put me through the wringer first. Throughout most of the night your message appeared to be: Don't need what I don't feel like giving.

Okay, now for emotions.

Last night after I'd hung up the final time I felt wide awake but mental: all steely brain. Except for two stabs of sharp, strong reaction. One was elation that we'd made it through the fight. The second was love, and wanting you, and feeling awful and deprived that you were gone, yet ashamed of longing for you. And as I started to write that last sentence I began to cry.

This morning I woke up feeling sharp and cold, like metal. I realized I was angry in a detached, icy way. I'm genuinely regretful that I can't greet you with my negative emotions dispelled. I should reward you for coming back at all, some voice in me warns. Yet it seems as if last night you'd said to me, "Stand on your own two feet" when I'd just broken my ankle. I envisioned acting cold for days to get back at you: the only revenge that seemed sufficient.

I've a sensation of burden. A load on my shoulders. And it's this: that I must take more than my share of initiative for what goes on between us. Right now I've a sense of wanting to skip, be free like a child, cast off caring for you, slough off the capacity to be hurt by you. Never mind wooing me. Being wooed is for women. When you won't pursue me you turn me into a child, dependent, on the short end of the string. Nix. I want off.

Shit. Not on you. Just shit.

Your pain-in-the-ass of a wife,
Mag

3. AN AGREEMENT

We agree to adopt as our base of operation with each other:

    1. "I" plus a verb expressing emotion does NOT mean "You should," or "You are."

    2. Judgings are subjective, irrelevant and undesirable; shoulds are crippling.

    3. All feelings are permissible, evident and aliveness to be shared whenever possible.

    4. Neither of us is better nor worse than the other; we're merely different.

    5. We owe one another nothing.

    6. Honesty is our best policy.

~ ~ ~ ~ ~ ~

Together we state:

We're not alive to suit the other's purposes, but to be ourselves. Inevitably we'll frustrate and pain one another, a fact for which we can feel regret but need suffer no guilt.

We acknowledge ourselves and each other to be healthy, whole individuals. Each of us trusts the other's honesty, self-knowledge and wisdom as equipping him/her to be the best judge and determiner of her/himself.

As much as possible we wish to afford one another tolerance, respect, acceptance, understanding and freedom. Failure to do so is permissible. We will attempt to admit our own lapses, and to react to the other's without accusation but with forgiveness and empathy. We hope in this way to unencumber the source of our relationship: love.

Psychology of Our Basic Fight
We both feel:

Adam
If you love me you wouldn't feel and express anger; invade my space.

Mag
If you love me you wouldn't withdraw; need space.

Adam
If you love me you wouldn't criticize my withdrawal so you needn't change your anger; thereby denying my right, and diminishing my space, to withdraw.

Mag
If you love me you wouldn't criticize my anger so you needn't change your withdrawal; thereby denying my right, and diminishing my space, to get angry.

Adam and Mag
I love you because with you I can....

Adam
....withdraw.

Mag
.... get angry.

View of the Basic Fight

Sequence
1. Mag: We're out of contact.
2. Adam: That's not my fault.
3. Mag: You're not owning your share.
4. Adam: You're attacking me.
5. Mag: You're cold.
6. Adam: You brought it on yourself

Mutual Goals
Contact, guiltlessness, validation, understanding, acceptance, reassurance, love.

Obstacles
Aroused guilt, into defensiveness, into accusation.

4. A SECOND LETTER

Dear Adam,

I can't continue to submit to your "double rejection" of me without suffering a loss of self-respect. It's not easy to say, "I'm needy of your friendship and your warmth. I hope my saying it might affect your feelings somewhat." My admission doesn't obligate you to respond. But my reaching out, sharing my vulnerability with you, running the risk of rejection, deserves respect—at least the tolerance of your refraining from finding my overture wanting while you continue unresponsive.

You've rejected me and blamed your rejection on my method of asking many times in the past, which is what I mean by "double rejection." You've a right to be any way you choose, but the time has come when I must protect myself from behavior that from my standpoint is destructive to me and to our relationship.

In the future I don't intend to tell you more than once that I want more from you than you seem at the moment desirous of giving. I'm speaking of when you're still angry with me (but I often can't tell if you are). I'm left today with the sense that the only way to avoid fights is for me to forego mention of any negative reactions to you or feelings about you.

It's not a question of who's right/wrong, who started what, who's to blame, etc. It's not that we've done anything dreadful—or at least not terribly dreadful. It's that in an intimate relationship the participants must work out a way of behaving that doesn't push the other person too far beyond his or her limits, prove too frustrating, etc. Well, our communication now, not just our fighting, is proving less and less workable for me.

I feel frightened and calm. I feel lonely, depressed, sad, grieving, but strong. I will not go down. On my own I'll release within me my old expectations—everyone has expectations, Adam, if they're alive or at all emotionally into a relationship. I'll find a way of relating to you that's not based on open communication. I see no other alternative.

But I feel as if I've lost my best friend. Because I have.

I'm not meaning to suggest that our partnership, our relating, is working any better for you than it is for me. In fact, I can only assume my frustration and discouragement are a measure of your own.

You tell me I don't accept your method of communicating. But do you fancy you accept mine? Last night you told me the reason you didn't want to hold hands at the festival was this: "You kept hinting. Why didn't you just take my hand?" And force on you a demonstration of affection IN PUBLIC, which you loathe? And having you holding my hand because you didn't dare withdraw? I made my wishes clear. If you object to my style of doing so, why not tell me at the time? But please don't kid yourself that you accept me either, as I am, and entertain no expectations of me. You had plenty of opinions on how I should let you know I wanted to hold hands.

Love,
Margaret (okay: Mag)

5. SECOND AGREEMENTS

We agree we'll exchange answers to:
    1. What is the point I'm fighting to make?
    2. What is the point I think you're fighting to make?
    3. What do I want you to give me now?
    4. What do I want to give and/or withhold from you now?

~ ~ ~ ~ ~ ~

Methods to Try for Stopping Fights
    1. Self-imposed by Mag: Don't, as Adam terms it, "yell." Attempt to become less assertive and more receptive when we're trying to cool a fight and communicate.
    2. Let's both of us try to ascertain what MESSAGES we're giving and receiving.
    3. When we're both angry, declare a period of silence during which we jot or write out notations if we've something we want to say. We can show or speak them to the other later, if we wish.
    4. We agree that if at bedtime either of us feels emotional hostility or distance is occurring between us, immediate negotiation of when we will attempt reconciliation is merited.
    5. Resume talk only when we both consider our own selves capable of hearing the other.
    6. When we're trying to feel friendly (again) before turning in, change the subject, not only from the fight but also from feelings about it.

Goals to Reach for
    1. To accept more deeply that emotions aren't right or wrong. So there's no need to justify them.
    2. To escape fault/blame, should/claim as frames of reference for either of us.
    3. To communicate for only "mutual understanding."

4. To accept that fighting, even when seemingly unavoidable, interferes with the attainment of our aims.

Procedure

Adam and Mag agree that her wish to resolve fights as fully as possible before bedtime is as valid as is his preference when he is very tired for going to sleep. He consequently can exercise choice, though not changeable during a quarrel, among these alternatives:

1. When an argument ends we exchange descriptions of our feelings either (a) verbally, or (b) in writing, he to decide which. Decisions to call it a night shall be mutual.

2. When Adam opts for sleep over Mag's protest, he spends that night on the living room couch. For twenty-four hours from the morning following the conflict no conciliation shall be expected of Mag.

The Bargain

TERMS

1. Adam's withdrawal is not from himself but from Mag. Consequently he isn't deadened by it.

2. Mag neither thinks Adam ought not to withdraw nor wishes to change him.

3. Adam is entitled to withdraw, and Mag is entitled to express anger, without stigmatization.

VIOLATION

When we betray the terms of our bargain we are hitting below the belt by:

1. Attempting to manipulate the other, to change him or her with rendering behavior unacceptable through shaming tactics;

2. Denying the other recognition of who s/he is.

We also are behaving humanly and permissibly.

6. A THIRD LETTER

Dearest Adam,

What do I mean when I say "I want...," you ask. When I use "I" followed by almost any feeling verb I'm informing you of what's going on in me. I do so partly to be known and accepted, if at all, for who and what I actually am, which I'm thereby owning up to. I'm announcing by implication that I stand behind my feelings as okay, not because they're necessarily "appropriate," but because they stem from me, an all-right person. I'm also acting out my conviction that true intimacy necessitates self-revelation that's as full and honest as possible. And I'm assuming that the giving of data about me is more helpful, at least in the long run, than the withholding of it.

When I speak out I'm psychically breathing. Emotions are energy. They require discharge if they're not to clog the psychological system. The mode of airing them that's natural to me is talking—or writing.

In other words, to summarize with a favorite phrase of mine these days, I'm "handling my end."

And, I insist, leaving you to handle yours. Your reaction doesn't concern me in advance, and when it occurs I want only to tell you what I think and feel about it. I'm setting out no specifications or conditions at all on what I consider acceptable feelings or behavior on your part. Nor am I asking you to meet standards of any kind for my sake. Neither am I insisting that you restrain yourself in any way so you don't "cause" reactions in me I find painful.

To attempt to persuade you to my way of viewing, affect your thought and emotion, is in my view strictly kosher. But only when I try to do so by presenting you with content valid to you. To strive to change or control you by arousing guilt feelings in you I consider a tactic of hitting below the belt. Nevertheless, though I'm responsible for whether or not I attempt to evoke remorseful reactions in you, only you are in charge of whether or not you experience them.

"I want" means only "I want," and not "I require of you." It's a remark to a peer, not to a child from a parent, and doesn't mean what a mother or father might intend.

What I primarily long for from you is your basing your reaction on the content of what I say, not on what you infer my motivation to be. I don't mind your commenting on my manner of presentation if you'll also acknowledge the effect on your thoughts and emotions of the overt substance of my remarks.

Statements starting with "I" instead of "you," especially with "I" plus feeling verbs, are to me tacit admission of the subjectivity of my experience and expression of it. I wish you'd reply or initiate in kind. If you can't, or won't, I love you anyway. But not everything about you all the time. I won't and can't require it of myself. Still, I wish only to have my present dislike—yes, even disapproval—accepted by you as part of, and valid for, me in the moment, and not as threat or command. You and you alone are responsible for and entitled to the establishing of what is required of you. Whenever I try to usurp your prerogative you've a right to cry "foul." I can only promise you my attempt to intimidate will prove transitory. For philosophically and from a long-range view, I want to support you as fully as possible in your gaining maximum inner freedom. As one step toward this goal of mine, I assure you again I put no conditions at all on my love for you and insist upon nothing from you in exchange for it. You've every right to react however you please and do. In any and every case, my emotional commitment to you is total.

With all my heart,
Mag

7. AN EXCHANGE

Adam and I this morning explored what goes awry in our communicating.

Adam

There's my case and yours, two among a possible many. I think we run into difficulty when we try to mesh them into a different third case. Each of us hears from the other, "You have no case." Each hears his own standpoint judged invalid by the other person. You and I feel our powers of perception and assessment are being attacked and undermined. At this point we both decide we're called upon to defend our own viewpoints to the nth degree.

Mag

Are you telling me what we want to hear from one another is, "You've a reasonable point of view?"

Adam

Yep, instead of attempting to find or construct the one correct case, I think each of us should try to understand our two cases, accepting both as reasonable and valid.

Mag

Are you suggesting it's not necessary to agree with one another, or concede that the other's case in any way invalidates one's own?

Adam

In fact, our cases need not be compared at all, but allowed to coexist roomily. I'm saying each of us needs to extend to the other the good will of believing the other's a reasonable person who'll present an acceptable case.

Mag

The third case may be necessary only when we need to reach a decision. And even then only at times.

Adam

I believe you talk an apple, say, and I hear orange, so your description sounds crazy to me because I think you're referring to the orange.

Mag

We try to blend an apple and an orange into apple/orange.

Adam

Not as mush but as a new fruit. We ought to assume the validity of the other's case as sort of an act of faith. Cases aren't irreconcilable. Our job is to find an area in the larger field of an issue where both our views are compatible.

8. A FOURTH LETTER

Dearest Adam,

You've asked me for a statement in writing, so you can refer back to it, of what I want most for myself in our relationship. I give it to you gladly. My primary wish is:

To be able to express my feelings, definitely including those that are negative, without your inferring any indirect message about how I think you "should" behave.

It's my strong impression you believe I become angry at, disapprove of or dislike only what I think should be changed. I honestly believe it isn't true of me.

When my feelings already exist, my only choice is whether to tell you openly what they are or show them to you indirectly and therefore confusingly. My purpose in offering reasons or explanations for them is merely to be as understandable to you as possible. How you respond to information I supply you is entirely up to you. Any request of you I make is for purposes solely my own and therefore doesn't obligate you to service me.

It's my conviction that my right to respond to you however I do constitutes a reproachful directive to you only if I think or claim I should have been spared the occurrence or my reaction to it.

As I see it, the actual situation between us isn't an either/or. It's my this and your that, and neither requires justification. When we realize what the case really is we give both of us room to breathe.

I hope I make sense to you.

All my love always,
Mag

9. A FIFTH LETTER

Dearest Adam,

I've decided to offer my further comments on our last set-to as a letter, so you can read it at leisure and give me a considered, rather than an immediate, response if you care to offer me any at all.

It's your interpretation of my words and actions, not they themselves, that causes your feelings. Till you're willing to tell me your inferences I can't possibly understand your judgments.

To think you needn't articulate them implies a belief that I already know them, one which constitutes your viewing your emotions as mirrors of my motivations, thoughts and intentions. Of course self-revelation is risky in that you may learn a cherished view of me is, at least from my standpoint, mistaken. So perhaps you figure if you don't want it challenged you'd better hide it where it's safe from scrutiny: in silence.

The more you attempt to shame me with labels the more resistance you evoke in me. Yet I like it when you're willing to take a specific stand instead of blurring your implications with generalities. These perhaps are designed to allow your ducking responsibility for meaning anything whatsoever it turns out I don't like.

I've a hunch you told yourself, "If she hadn't gotten on my case and upset me I'd have figured out right away how to tape the compact disks." To me, "my case" represents the claim that if you don't know what to do I should offer no comment threatening to your pride in your competence.

But these days I've no intention of disappearing into the woodwork as the sexist, "helpless" woman whose only concern should be protecting the male ego from any blow. I'm no longer willing to collude in continuing the charade. In the past I've contributed my share in its perpetuation, one equal to yours. But this role infantilizes

157

me and prevents my developing competence of my own with mechanical apparatus.

You told me, "I'm sorry I got so mad." I believe you've a truly vested interest in viewing me as difficult in situations involving equipment. Your probable reaction, to my mind, we all share in one or another way as we grow older. It's: "What's the matter with me? Am I losing my mental grip on the world?" My answer about you: "No more than any of the rest of us, your contemporaries."

It's frightening and sad for all of us to suspect or feel our powers are waning. We're thrown back to the Vulnerable Child inside of us all. These are reactions you could entrust to me without implanting ideas in my head that they're factual. I don't mean to be a pollyanna; all I can offer as consolation is: As all of us age we at least can attempt, and manage somewhat, we hope, to grow wiser; meaning, less invested in the rightness of our own judgments.

You later commented that this image occurs to you: I listen to you from the side of myself who's my Vulnerable Child, but speak to you as my Witch. My answering thought is that in all likelihood the Witch appears to protect the Child. You generously added that probably you, too, present yourself in dual role.

It seems to me your insight is one of those rich intuitions full of implications beyond the moment's applicability. You suggest that two or more aspects of personality can operate simultaneously, yet fulfilling different functionings. They then can divide the overall field of activity between or among themselves.

Thank you, Adam, for this enlightening contribution to our communications.

> With my best love always,
> Mag

10. JOURNALISMS: ONE

[I offer none of the book's following material as a diary. I instead create from actualities a journal depicting two persons. Although undated, I present entries in roughly the chronological order of their occurrence. Almost throughout I focus on largely a central conflict within a synthesized marriage.

Why didn't I record happy events? Merely the living of them seemed to pay them sufficient homage. Even so, what was my reason for attending primarily to misunderstandings and quarrels? In the hope of gaining more comprehension of their causes. Admittedly this pound of cure often failed to produce the ounce of prevention. Hope nevertheless dangles as the carrot. Other aspects, therefore, of frequently untroubled relationship I bypass to favor the clarity of an uncluttered perspective.]

~ ~ ~ ~ ~ ~

(April 16th)

I told Adam I ask only this: to be allowed expression of my views, have him listen to them and afford me the respect of giving them courteous and serious consideration. He then can react according to the merits, as he sees them, of the case I present. And if this requirement pressures him too much for him to view it other than as an attempt to control, I may not want to live here anymore.

He replied it's not overbearing, he's crazy to claim it is, it's unfair. He admitted he feels pressured by what I say and wants to shut me up, permanently change the subject. His reason is at least partly his fear of succumbing to his own need for accommodating other people.

(three months later)

I admitted to Adam I sometimes can bear no longer the sameness of the emotional tone between us. After days and days of plateau I need to make waves.

(fourteen months later)

I think I must switch my goal from communicating to articulation, mine. I can't be responsible for his response. I can only do the best I can to my own satisfaction.

(eleven months later)

Barring a miracle, I shall never have with him what I most want: a situation where I can express negative feelings without his hearing accusation where and when none is intended.

The momentary understandings, so slight in comparison with the amount of struggle necessary to attain them, don't yield any progress the next time.

I told him if the situation between us doesn't improve I think we should consider seriously whether we wouldn't be better off separating.

(six months later)

Maybe I can just focus on, as my aim, expressing myself as honestly and effectively as I can to my own satisfaction. Which doesn't imply I can't and won't react emotionally to how he responds, and say so, as part of being honest. It means I don't hang in there explaining over and again, and not giving up because he doesn't get it, misinterprets, etc.

If I base my evaluations on myself and how I account for myself (charitably allowing myself room to mess up) rather than on results I have with him, I'll feel less that I've failed after intense effort and less frustrated.

My goal must switch not just to self-expression but to self-understanding, to a clarification of my position for my own sake.

(one week later)

One possibility that really scares me is: I don't want to become ashamed of and lose my spontaneity. I'm afraid that if I begin to monitor too closely how I speak, what I say, how, in other words, I express my feelings, I'll begin to watchdog my emotions themselves. Even inside myself. And from my psychoanalysis on I've fought too hard a battle for the right to my own feelings to risk tossing out my victory now, at this late date.

Can I, then, allow myself initial freedom, and, next, backtrack and acknowledge my probable effect, verifying what portions of it I stand behind or refute?

(two weeks later)

I want to unhook from having to affect him a certain way. Until I can, I'm clearly not my own person. His reactions, not mine, control my sense of success, efficacy. Do I want to give him this power over me, this power from within me? As long as my goal is a specific, predetermined and set result about anything whatsoever, I've projected myself onto the outside, disowned that piece of me.

~ ~ ~ ~ ~ ~

I realize part of me can't bear to give up the fights because I fear our entire relationship will become bland and superficial without them.

(four months later)

My grief is the sadness of being thought badly of; and of being told I say and do what I don't. Example: The accusation that I've given him a "big bawling out" when I've not admonished him about anything with "You shouldn't have."

I don't think I can ever unhook from him, his judgment of me, as long as my goal is to change that judgment, rather than merely to evaluate it for myself.

(two weeks later)

Today I told Adam I want more than anything to be able to love him as much as I know I'm capable of. But when I can't respect his fairness and objectivity I seem unable to. I thought yesterday I won't expect it of myself. And what will I substitute for the pleasure? Living the present moment to the full, whatever its content may be. Allowing myself to become as totally involved as I please in other matters. Accept "It would be very nice if...," yet not cast a pall on what life has to offer by brooding about what isn't and what I can't control. All the same, I feel sad today.

(one week later)

Why do I want to unhook from investing so much intensity—rage— and efforts to persuade in my reactions to Adam? Do I really and truly wish to detach from the outcomes of our encounters? The side of me that longs to feel in love says no. Another part, the me who wants independence and autonomy, declares yes.

(six weeks later)

But in all honesty (never mind shoulds), why is it I want to unhook? I'm tired of rising to his bait, feeling like a puppet on a string he pulls. I crave to get back at him, give him a taste of his own medicine—

withdrawal—and a mouthful of feeling impotent, out of control of one's circumstances and scene. I want to rise above him, and look down on him, as an expression of fury.

I want to shame him by "behaving well" as a new attempt to get what I long for. I've an image of stepping aside to let him fall flat on his face. I wish, in simple English, to refuse playing what has become, as I view it, his present game. I'd like to be able to state more frequently and quietly "I don't agree with your perception and I'm sorry you feel as you do about it." Then let the matter go at that.

It isn't just a case of not wishing to dance to his tune, of not wanting to waste time and energy futilely and knowingly. On a deeper level I long for my freedom from having his reactions and/or my anticipation of them condition my choices and behaviors. I yearn to choose them for their own sake and for reasons other than trying to buy his good opinion. It's okay to want it but not to mar the honesty of my representation of who I really am in order to get it. Mar it either to myself or with him.

I covet the liberty from caring about his opinion (which is different from not caring about him, himself) sufficiently to know and be myself. I want to give myself the strength of recognizing I'm being me no matter what, that I won't pay the price of misrepresenting myself for the sake of any relationship whatsoever.

I aspire no longer to needing his image of me for informing me of who I am.

11. JOURNALISMS: TWO

(one day later)

The danger in relying on self-estimations is that of becoming inflated with a self-righteous belief in one's infallibility of judgment. I hope for no decision rights with Adam. Let me persuade on the merits of my case. But I think it's utterly unrealistic to expect success. He's more apt to be defensive than open, at least for now. It's the way he is, or the way people are, or how I come across to him.

Yet I don't want to detach emotionally from Adam, lose my positive feelings for him. I'd like continuing the capacity to feel in love with him, even if not on my former basis. So I now had better recognize and accept that a part of him is what I don't, and needn't, even like about him. I then must allow myself both deep negative feelings and emotional vulnerability, which means I must be prepared to experience much pain at times. If I'm willing to, I may be able to "have it all," meaning sometimes, and only then, the sense of being in love, and joyousness, lightheartedness, about it.

I cannot care for him truly as any kind of projection of me, but as a separate and unique individual who is thus and so, some of which is pleasing to me, who is another thus and so, and some of which offends me.

I also think I must choose to be here with him not on the basis of love alone. He thereby becomes my lot on earth, life's challenge to me, and to abandon it, him, would be to shrivel because I've denied myself the chance to grow. To conflict with another human being in and to the depths of one's soul is to find out who one is, and to become one's newer self within the smelting pot, the kiln, the cauldron, of happening.

And yet I can't make staying with him no matter what an absolute either. To do so would be to attempt rigidifying our situation, restricting it artificially by setting boundaries, closing exits, denying myself my in-the-present's choice.

To stay or leave is a decision, different from the wish, bred by the moment, to do either. And as long as I'm still here I want to count him too, understand, sympathize, accept as much as I'm able, and be aware of my feelings in any one moment.

Yesterday morning I told him with considerable force that I love him because we have, and partly because he permits, communication in which I can say to him, as I just had, "I deeply resent..."

I aim for a relationship in which I allow him his right to be himself as much and deeply and widely as I want to permit myself this liberty. A marriage in which I understand his right to his reactions. Their purpose is not to serve my goals and need not be, no matter how much I dislike his stands, can't respect them and am hurt by them. A partnership in which I strive to be as honest with myself and with him as possible, and am willing in doing so to let the chips fall where they may.

I've a right to evaluate myself irrespectively of his judgments, with which I'm entitled to disagree. I no longer need infer or feel that if he thinks ill of me he must be correct, accurate, factual in doing so. I needn't decide that since he loves me he desires to think well of me, and would if I gave him the opportunity. I'm accepting that his judgments of me serve his purposes, not mine, and that his are often, for the moment at least, not those of our relationship: they're intrapsychic, not interpersonal.

More and more I'm really feeling "this too shall pass," so the happy times must be experienced as good while and if we can and the troublesome lived and accepted as what they are: bad. We'll never reach the point of putting the disagreeable behind us. If and when we do we'll have jelled and thereby died.

(four months later)

My heart beat became very irregular. Adam appeared unconcerned. I protested his avoidance of trouble and his stance of "not crossing bridges." He broke in sarcastically with "thanks for the psychology lecture." He later apologized rather unemotionally. My heart regained its normalcy.

Part of what made me so mad is not only his image of me as lecturing but also his using the label to shut me up. I'm also angry with him for asking "what's wrong with lecturing?". For him plenty is wrong with it, at least at the time he makes his accusation.

I told him his apologies aren't very effective with me now because he's name-called with the same labels so many times I feel those tags constitute his mental image of me, ready to be popped into use when they suit his purposes. These days once the incident is over I await the next occasion.

I'm not required to love anyone whose judgments of me I consider harsh, based on distortions of reality, unloving and unloveable. I'm accepting my right not to care deeply for him no matter how much he might attempt to persuade or shame me into it, no matter how "unaccepting" he may call me.

He has every right to any image of me he wishes. And I've just as much right to hate it, be angered by it; yes, and judge it, and to withdraw from him because of it. I can simply feel and say "I don't want to feel close and loving toward anyone who has this picture of me, who treats me to this kind of labelling. It's not acceptable to me in an intimate relationship."

I've a sense that of this incident, moment, my love for him has changed. I told him I no longer guarantee sexual fidelity.

(four months later)

Lately I've eperienced a certain freedom, glimpsing it as I would a light at the end of a tunnel (which I'm now in). It stems from foreseeing not—yes, not—being in love with Adam or even allowing him still the centrality in my emotional life, or just plain my life, as I gave him formerly. I have revelled in my romance with him and I grieve and have mourned the loss of it. All the same, I may find I'm more my own person when I'm not invested in "hanging in" until we attain some bit of understanding in each particular situation.

I predict for the future far less concern on my part with his opinion of me, with pleasing him. I plan to focus on behaving as a decent person in ways I can approve. I hope I won't as willingly deny that a projection on his part is exactly that and not controllable by me. My behavior doesn't cause it and changing my speech and actions won't cure it. My summary is this: I'm ready to move on.

(three weeks later)

I asked Adam if he wanted intimacy. He said yes, without it he'd feel lost, and his voice broke; he was crying. Maybe it got to me, I don't know. My speech had been quiet and continued so. I told him I think we must assume we're strangers, very different people.

We need to forget the past and all our preconceptions as much as possible, then listen freshly to each other, like we're acquaintances who've just met. He agreed. That night, yesterday, we made really passionate love. Something has changed. I feel tears rising as I write.

I'd like to try to know him, understand him, as he is, let him alone to be what he is and love him for it, whenever and to the extent that I'm able then to feel warm at all.

(six months later)

I told Adam I felt hurt that he didn't ask me to marry him on our engagement anniversary as he used to. He replied he didn't know where he stood, was trying to get into his feelings. I held out my hand and told him, "I want you back." He replied he considered it a very controlling statement full of strings and conditions. Next day he did apologize. But he accused me of blaming him, making him responsible, for my feelings. His amplification: If he hadn't made such and such a remark, or done so and so, I wouldn't have felt hurt.

(six weeks later)

Whether or not I'm accusing, attacking, lecturing, criticizing, trying to control, etc. isn't actually the issue anymore. At least not for me. It's impossible to express any kind of negative reaction without criticizing to some extent, at least by implication. It's a matter of degree. As far as my conscious motivation is concerned, I'm not attempting to change his stands or him, himself. And I'm the one who has the right to be spokesperson for myself. Adam is no more objective about my unconscious than I am; he's just as invested in seeing me his way.

(seven weeks later)

Adam and I had a bit of a set-to about his interrupting me. I relinquished any attempt, by continuing an explanation of my point of view, to influence its outcome. I asked him his emotions; he replied, "resentful" at having had his lesson for the day. Suddenly I didn't care what his reaction was. I expressed sincere regret that he'd experienced me as lecturing. I didn't feel angry or guilty. My involvement, investment, in our exchange drained from me. I felt friendly toward him, relaxed, even loving. He volunteered that having spoken of his annoyance he felt it a lot less strongly. He put his arms around me and gave me a warm kiss which I returned. He then thanked me for not becoming angry. I assured him he needn't; I just didn't happen to. The incident leaves me with a very good feeling.

12. JOURNALISMS: THREE

(four months later)

I confess that a side of me would rather assume fault in order to feel in control than accept I'm not and enjoy my actual innocence. But I also don't like appeals to guilt. I want to present my arguments (that is, points of view) and have them considered on the basis of their own merits.

Yet I've never before had such a gut realization that I'm not in charge of anyone else, including Adam, whether or not he knows it. I may not be innocent of wanting or even trying to control, but I am, nevertheless, innocent of controlling. I can only affect another person in ways he or she allows.

So it really isn't important from a "practical" standpoint whether or not, or to what degree, I'm trying to change Adam, since my success or lack of it is up to him.

What I can't approve of in myself is dishonesty for the purpose of manipulation. True expression of my feelings, thoughts, interpretations, judgments (admitted as such) is okay with me.

(two months later)

For living with Adam, I need to change goals and premises. My aim must be honesty, speaking for my self-respect and to own my own truth, to hear what I have to say. It should no longer be to communicate. I need to accept that in part, at least, Adam wants not to hear negatives. Justification of this stance will somewhat color all his reactions. These render it foolish and unproductive of me to continue explaining myself. I hope to keep my focus on what I wish to say, and not let it slip over to his reactions.

(one month later)

Driving us, I ran a stop sign. Adam asked if I normally do so. I told him I'd like him to express his feelings and criticisms directly instead of resorting to sarcasm. We fell into silence. Later I told him I was available for reconciliation. He replied that I didn't sound like it, adding "I can't get through your wall of anger". I held out both my hands and asked him "You call these a wall of anger?" His resistances broke down and we ended up in our bedroom, he holding me.

But today, what a reaction. I'm furious that I leave myself in the position of his continuing to reject, insisting all the while he wants us to get back together but I'm making it impossible. And I argue. Why don't I understand he's compelled to interpret the situation as he does? It appears to me he isn't ready to admit that he's still angry. Consequently he needs to justify his emotions as reactions to my behavior, perceiving it as the obstacle to a reconciliation he's attempting to achieve.

I also realize I feel responsible, partly because I'm a woman, for getting us back together. My premise is that I should meet him more than halfway. As I told Adam, I don't accept that responsibility anymore.

I'm not forced to persuade him I want to reconcile. I'm not required to lay myself open to his rejections which "add insult to injury": He not only spurns my overtures but declares I'm at fault that he does so because of my manner in offering peace. I needn't necessarily pull off a successful making-up. I can just let it hurt and scare me that I failed. After set-to's we either get back together or we don't. I will honor my feelings of that time, not behave as I think I should. I at least can conduct myself with some self-protectiveness and dignity.

I also just confessed to Adam I can't forgive us for our mutual pain until I can act as I want to.

(five months later)

We agree that if I say to him "I'd like to be close again when you're ready" he will consider the statement an overture. He will respond in terms of his own wishes of the moment, rather than with his usual analysis of my intent. At this point I hope I'll deal with the message I'm getting: He isn't ready to return emotionally, so wants the offer to go away. Then I can either leave it or withdraw it

(six months later)

Adam admits he doesn't recognize a reaching out when for any reason he doesn't with to. He asks that I clearly preface it with the announcement that I'm making one, and with the remark that he can reject it, accept it, or take time to consider it, but please not attack it.

169

(two months later)

I think I now really understand how little Adam wants me to express any reaction that's negative no matter what he declares to the contrary. Consequently I'm speaking out for me, not him. And I must, or I destroy the relationship for myself.

I'm beginning to accept our deep differences and the inevitable incompatibilities they yield much more thoroughly than I did formerly. And the ensuing loneliness. I'm truly starting to get the point: Never the twain shall meet.

(six months later)

Adam announced that when I tell him "you hurt me" or even "I'm hurt by what you said or did" I'm in effect demanding "change, damn you, change." I replied "no way" and reminded him I'd spent many hours striving to express my perspective and philosophy on the subject. All to no avail. But I object to his not believing what I say about myself. He's setting himself up as a more knowledgeable authority than I on what goes on in me, which is arrogant.

(three months later)

I suddenly feel we're both equally caught in the web of our basic incompatibility: the woman who wants and needs to talk and the man who doesn't wish to hear, needs not to. I quickly felt a strong rush of love for us both. A wave of sympathy for Adam engulfed me. I found myself in his shoes. What a basically good person he is! Later came grief for myself, a lot.

(three months later)

We quarrel. He delayed paying bills for financial reasons without discussing the postponement with me. My fear I voice to Adam is: He wants closeness as the price he must pay for a relationship with me. Once he withdraws, left to his own devices he'd stay away emotionally forever if I don't come after him. This is the "truth" I've been afraid to discover, so I've pursued him. I'm now ready to let happen what will. Adam lovingly reassured me my anxiousness is baseless.

(three months later)

I feel in a new place. Deep serenity goes with it. I sense I've experienced a psychological satori.

For the first time I really seem to know what's Adam and what's me. The boundaries between us are clear. Maybe now I'm in a space some persons describe as "centered."

My existence is absolute. It isn't conditional upon meeting any standard, expectation, should. It is within; all else is without. What I am, as I am, is not a relative.

Adam's judgments are facts of him, not facts of me. My reactions are facts of me, not of him. The facts in space are only the tangibles: sounds, vibrations, sights, etc.

I feel disidentified from Adam. And so I'm a one of the many. I'm also a one of the One.

I think in the future I'll care what are Adam's feelings about me, but not undergo concern with his judgments. Both are not-me in a psychological sense, though of course from a metaphysical perspective we're in union.

(four months later)

I told Adam that whatever he says is information about himself; whatever I say is information about me. And that's absolutely all both are. At least in my opinion.

13. JOURNALISMS: FOUR

(six weeks later)

We made sensational love. During and afterward I experienced a total high stronger than any of recent years. I was deliriously happy. I later asked Adam if his emotions were at all similar. He said no. I felt devastated, that our love is old and I don't have it for him anymore. I requested that he listen to me, hearing no criticism but merely information about me. I moved closer to him. He nervously put one hand on my shoulder. I put my arms around him and for a few moments held him very close. I asked his reactions. He replied it seemed to him I'd crushed his balls off. I said I was sorry.

When I questioned him about what causes him to feel castrated he informed me, "When you criticize me." And how criticized? His response: "Merely raising an issue is always a rebuke." At this point I realized fully what I'm still up against.

(six months later)

Adam seems to me relatively guilt-free about his thoughts and feelings. It's his actions about which he becomes defensive. I infer they determine for him whether or not he's behaving as, and therefore being, Mr. Good Husband.

(one week later)

Adam volunteered this opinion: He believes it's his fault if we have a fight, then can't stand the guilt, so to both of us he makes me the culprit. I responded that his control side wants all responsibility, while his moral part campaigns for none. He appeared to listen and stated "I think I'm beginning to catch on." I don't dare hope, much less trust. But he was very loving afterward.

(two days later)

This realization dawns on me: When Adam understands why I express so-called negatives I've pulled the rug from under him. I've invalidated his feeling criticized and consequently castrated him.

(three weeks later)

I believe that for Adam the negative feeling itself and/or its articulation is the "beating" he often cites. In viewing it as such he robs me of an inalienable right in an intimate relationship: to express myself and have that behavior considered acceptable.

(one week later)

Adam becomes particularly defensive when he feels in some way inconsiderate.

(three weeks later)

Adam's and my ideas of intimacy are widely different. I'm convinced at least part of him believes that if I truly loved and accepted him I'd understand him and therefore not become angry with him. Or if I do I'd elect not to voice my ire.

(one day later)

I predict we'll never rid ourselves of fights. My impression is that I'm gaining in emotional aloofness, self-sufficiency, when we lock horns. Yet I don't want to come at myself with reproaches if I'm not detached enough to suit me.

Adam's contribution: It's not a case of how we word what we say according to rules. He claims he desires to operate with no strictures; let it all hang out for us to muddle through.

Adam can be a true dear.

I firmly believe the only solution for us is to fight. But perhaps we can avoid becoming emotionally more riled up than is necessary.

Once again I reminded him: He needn't adjust one thing about himself for my sake, or to keep me happy and loving him. Just as he is he's utterly acceptable to me in whole and in part. I don't require of either of us that I like and approve of everything about him. I can fully accept what I dislike and wish were different without thinking it should change. I want only this right when my reactions are negative: to admit my feelings about what to me are the less loveable aspects of him.

(one day later)

Adam announced a breakthrough for himself. He realizes that when rules go, so do fault/blame, right/wrong, incorrect/correct because there's no longer any measurement. So anything and all become acceptable.

I feel very happy and loving of him. I still believe that times will occur when I need/want to talk and he needs/wants me silent.

(three weeks later)

I noted earlier that what I need to say he needs not to hear. Resulting attitudinal and emotional conflicts and incompatibilities are sad for both of us. He announced this morning, holding me, that he's very much in love with me. That we still can connect on a feeling level is a tribute to the adaptability, acceptingness, tenacity and courage—both to stand ground and to face unpleasant truths—of both of us. He agreed.

14. JOURNALISMS: FIVE

(one week later)

Adam and I checked the phones to ascertain which was out of commission. I discovered he'd made notations in ballpoint on all extensions. I told him I didn't feel critical, just bothered, yet in the future I'd appreciate his not marking joint property indelibly without checking with me first. He rejoined in a loud and vehement voice, "You're picking on me. You're telling me what to do." I announced my disagreement with him. He apologized, then stated I'd been nasty and almost snarling. From my standpoint I'm almost certain I wasn't. He complained that I'd found fault with his system of testing the phones and gone on and on about it. I rejoined with fervor that I disagreed. He retorted with, "I feel picked on right this moment."

I've kind of a Zen-like feeling now. Accepting when I've lost the struggle to get through to him, I can give it up. My degree of investment in our relationship needn't be fixed. It can fluctuate, just like my distancing may, according to circumstances.

I can retire into myself whenever I please and not concern myself with results. I intend to give myself the right to retreat as deeply and for as long as I wish. If I'm able I shan't feel guilty about depriving him of closeness. I'll try not to worry too much about my motivation: am I seeking revenge, control, etc. I hope to let go of all attempt at changing anything that's happening in him. I also can release myself from all obligation to feel a certain way about him: to be in love with him, to remain committed to communication and connectedness, whatever.

I thereby can loosen myself, I trust, from all involvement with my effect on this man. All I need do is believe at last what to me has seemed with the passing of time more and more obvious: I've no control over what he thinks or feels. I'm indeed powerless to change any of it according to my wishes. Whenever I'm giving him "a hard time" I might as well stop talking because I accomplish nothing by continuing. I can then withdraw into...myself. I'll still l have me.

(one day later)

I suspect he sees us in a battle for survival and is convinced that if he doesn't win it, he loses it. No such thing as a draw.

(one week later)

I no longer will consider myself the cause of Adam's emotions. Regardless of whether or not I am indeed the effector of his feelings, I refuse to assign myself this task: changing his situation to a more pleasant one, or one more tolerable or beneficial to me. I shall evaluate my own behavior however I please. I no longer feel that in doing so I'd assume self-righteousness as long as I allow this: His judgment of me is the appropriate one for him to hold. If not, it's his business, not mine.

Adam and I are in accord: My frame of reference is suitable for me, the whole of who I am; his isn't. And his is suitable for him in his totality; mine is not.

(six months later)

Adam and I quarreled because he hadn't made arrangements for inspection of our burglary alarm system. I learned I'm in a new place and am I ever feeling gratified about it. At first I was angry, partly because of charges he'd leveled. I weighed them and decided I didn't agree with him. I felt okay about my behavior. Clearly he'd distanced himself, and I simply went into my own space. I continued with my daily life, inner and outer, without anxiety or a need to effect or rush a change in the status of matters between us. I didn't feel he'd gotten to me in the sense of taking over my consciousness, nor did I find myself wishing to argue or attempt to change his mind. I'd had my say and however he reacted was his business. I no longer experienced myself as his captive or at his emotional beck and call, nor was I tempted to justify myself on his turf, or even at all.

What I felt, I realize, is loose from him and therefore free. Not non-caring or uncommitted but for the time being uninvolved because so was he and I could stand it, thank you, very well indeed. This morning I was guarded but not irate, nor did I feel critical, guilty or accountable to him—this despite his accusing me of trying to control him, etc. and turn him into my puppet. I saw his attitude as his stance, and because it was quite predictable it also seemed to me rather funny. God, I felt, and still feel liberated, like I'm breathing much fresh air.

(three weeks later)

I told Adam I wished not to accept a bracelet as an anniversary gift if he didn't care to help me shop for it. He could get me something else or nothing, I'd buy the bracelet as just a replacement of the other, stolen, an earlier anniversary present. I admitted I felt hurt that he wasn't interested in helping to buy his remembrance to me.

He accused me of barking at him, yet I was quite careful to speak quietly. He also complained I was expecting him to fix my emotions. He'd heard my message: He has all sorts of problems which he ought to get rid of and then I'd be fine.

I really felt in my gut our inability to communicate through to an understanding concerning negative feelings. Next, I experienced a lancing joy followed by a feeling/thought: "I'm rescued" from the need for trying to explain myself, from responsibility for his emotions, opinions, reactions, to me. A calm resignation followed: I accepted the loneliness, aloneness, of not being understood (at least by Adam). I also lost hope of his comprehending me in that there's nothing I can do toward bringing about rapport. I suspect, though, I've another session to go through of grieving.

Moments ago Adam stated that, yes, he believes that a person's expression of anger to the person toward whom he feels it is an attempt to control. Not so, necessarily, of the feeling itself. He's decided he gave up his childhood rage when he no longer needed to manipulate. I reminded him he once had admitted his inner victory required his burial of the feeling of anger itself.

I assured him I don't wish to live in self-denial. I protested I couldn't disagree with him more thoroughly that stating anger is in itself proof of a wish to control. It may and it may not be. I explained that I visualize a spectrum. At one pole, the refusal even to try for any effect; at the other, an all-out attempt to achieve it totally. At center, the acknowledgment aloud of one's self, meaning one's inner experience. Further to the right, the attempt to persuade, but by the content of one's argument, not with attacks on the person one would win over. Effort, and permissible attempt are matters of degree.

I've lost all trust in his ever understanding where I'm coming from. And he's renounced his hope of my agreeing that, yes, I'm trying to change him and therefore infringing on his rights when I vent my mad. But at least we've laid out this basic difference in terms neither of us can deny any longer.

I'm rather proud of both of us that we've tried as long and hard as we have to reach a meeting of minds, one which would allow us at least some understanding of one another's basic issues. It's time, though, to quit because we accomplish zilch. I'm glad to listen to him whenever he wishes to speak about himself. I'll say what I can for his sake to rectify if possible his sense of being attacked for faults, and that's it.

(three days later)

I confronted Adam with our much earlier exchange about his withdrawals. He asked me at that time to stop branding them neurotic since they're a truly major part of him. I conceded I should change my judgment and I did. Expressiveness of my feelings is as basic to me as shutting down is to him. I don't think he affords me the tolerance, respect, good faith I granted him.

I questioned Adam about what he wants from me when he tells me I'm trying to control him. He replied that he'd like my agreement. I warned him he won't get it from me, which he admitted he realizes.

(three weeks later)

I quietly asked Adam if he'd try to hear what it's like inside my skin. With his constant charges that I express my feelings in order to have a certain effect on him, here's what his message as far as I'm concerned implies: Though my emotions are vitally me, I've no respect for them, but am willing to use them as manipulatory tools. He said he thought he understood somewhat, but I felt very sad.

Attempting not to let his very basic misunderstanding of me, as I view it, alter my love or romantic feelings, or detract in the least for me from our relationship, is simply more of a burden than I can handle. I can't ask of myself that I "rise above it" or "grow beyond it" to the point that I react negatively only temporarily. I cannot try to be that "noble." His image of me does make a difference, by God, whether or not it should. And with this inner confession I feel just as sorrowful still, but considerably lighter.

I find him judgmental. And I wish to be, too, at the moment: When he considers his emotions are mere reflections of another's motivation, on the one hand he's implying he doesn't independently exist: he's passive putty. Yet he's also self-aggrandizing. His implication is that he's so objective, uncontaminated, psychologically healthy, etc., he couldn't have added his "stuff" when he reacts—oh, no—but only reflects as a mere pool of scene. To assume he knows me better than I know myself is mind rape. I told him he's in my psychic space. "Who's in whose space?" he bellowed. "From my standpoint," I replied, "you're in mine."

Adam and I do indeed invade each other's inner territory. He judges my motivation, then considers his conclusions to be facts. I inflict my noisiness on him with the insistence that he attend to it. I also attempt in my own behalf to undermine his defenses unfavorable to me.

We agreed that in terms of joint space his has expanded and mine has shrunk.

I might add that he's more assertive and I'm more detached. The day he initiates a discussion about some negative feeling of his, a dislike, makes a request, etc. I'll know we've passed as ships in the night, to be trite.

15. JOURNALISMS: SIX

(four days later)

Adam announced he's decided that I accept him but he doesn't match my forebearance. I admitted I consider the statement true at this stage of our relationship.

He volunteered that as a fourth-grade youth he decided to fight on the playground in self-protection only. Then he felt frustrated in expressing anger and so less free. The only way he could consider himself in charge was not to experience rage at all unless he could vent it. And now, to feel justified in strongly articulating negative emotions he must label them survival techniques. He even conceded he can't express wants except defensively.

~ ~ ~ ~ ~ ~

I stated that my requests of him are two: (1) Don't tell me my motivation; (2) Refrain from offering your judgments of me as facts.

(five days later)

Adam declared he wants to change his attitudes to accommodate my expressions of negative feelings. I asked why, and he replied that he likes emotional contact and now believes negatives are as important to achieving and maintaining it as positives are. I shall see what results, perhaps testing in a gingerly fashion. I don't expect an immediate miracle.

(four months later)

I told him I consider his labeling a device to change the subject, to which he replied, "Of course."

Suddenly I'd a sense of snipping cords between Adam and me, of his being a completely separate person, one utterly acceptable, dear, simply as "what-is". I felt as if I'd withdrawn all my projections onto him. I also experienced myself as an adult, able to care for myself. I began to cry, then also to laugh. It was all an "aha!" occurrence.

When I tried to explain it to Adam he remarked that to him it sounded like rebirth, and that I'd cut the cord. I shouted "Of course! The umbilical cord! Thank you! Now you needn't be the mother anymore who nurtures me." And I wept again.

(three months later)

Adam revealed to us both that he likes to fight, having denied himself the privilege from the fourth grade on until he married me.

(one month later)

Adam has become noticeably nondefensive. When I've expressed any kind of negative reaction I've also, at the end of my presentation, told him exactly what response I'd like from him. I've watched his face visibly relax when I give him an idea of what he can do to remedy my situation (if not his). I suppose he no longer need feel guilty because he's been told all is fixable.

In any case, I afford him a clearcut choice when I explain my wishes: He can accede to them or not. He's not left to flounder in an amorphous mass of articulated emotion. I do attempt, however, to make clear he's in my view entitled to decide in terms of his own feelings and self-interest.

(six weeks later)

Adam and I again are at crossroads in terms of intimacy. Years ago he asked me to stop considering withdrawal a neurosis and I changed my attitude. Now I'm making a similar request of him. He then inquired whether I were driving a bargain. I replied no, I'd put no conditions on altering my position at the time, had complied unilaterally, so now lack all medium of exchange. I can only petition. And what I desire is that he stop considering all feelings and thoughts about him which are negative to be also this judgment: He's in the wrong in some fashion and should change.

About matters I believe he'll react defensively to, I'm more frequently expressing myself only when my integrity demands it, which is less and less often. Our interpersonal world of intimacy is shrinking for me.

He seems convinced that if I really accept him as he is, consider him okay, I'd experience no negative reactions to him whatsoever. But he hides awareness of this premise, which rationally he can't quite justify. So he tells himself it's the way I present my case, not its content, to which he responds angrily. But he has yet to answer my requests that he explain to me how I could have worded my statements in a manner satisfactory to him.

He now claims he plans to change his positions in ways I'm asking for. We shall see.

(three days later)

Adam agrees with me that he doesn't think any negative feeling of his is justified unless I intend to produce it, and it exactly.

(four days later)

It occurs to me that Adam's bargain with The Fates probably is this: If he doesn't initiate difficulties with others he deserves that they not instigate problems with him (including evoking his negative emotions). And my myth? I should elicit only the mental image of me that I've earned or merit. In other words, if I behave decently I'm entitled to be thought well of by my significant other.

(four days later)

I'm willing to share with you who I am, but not be who you want me to be.

16. JOURNALISMS: SEVEN

(nine weeks later)

I do think Adam and I will continue to fight. What I need to say is what he needs not to hear, and vice versa. Different parts of me will be out when various conflicts begin, so I'll spontaneously react uniquely for each episode. I don't think I can formularize and also behave inwardly and outwardly in a genuine way. I'll just have to let happen what does, in my feelings, thoughts and actions. This realization spells uncertainty, is therefore rather uncomfortable and provoking of anxiety. So be it.

(ten weeks later)

Adam interrupted me, I protested, he defended his right to do so, I disagreed, and he showed me his arm, implying "Look how you're beating on me" or "Come on; beat on me." He also told me I'd repeated myself twenty-three times. I laid out just how I feel about it all, so I'm fairly satisfied with the outcome. In the process of resolving the set-to I told him I think he struck this unilateral bargain with life: In exchange for no criticism he won't make negative waves. So his angers require justification as totally defensive. He asked my bargain. I rejoined with: I'll earn approval, thereby neutralizing all fault-finding of me, past and present.

(one week later)

I told Adam I know in my gut I've crossed some kind of boundary, Rubicon, and reached a different place, saying it tearfully and feeling humbly grateful. My main "symptom," mood-wise, is buoyancy that's trouble-free. I think I've really dropped the sense that my judgments have any kind of objective validity, mean anything except as indications of what I am. And when nothing is judged wrong, all is okay, no fixing is required. So there's no need for control, and consequently no anxiety over not having it.

As long as I'm invested in results of stances I adopt with him—emotional and rational—my center of gravity occurs outside myself, in him, and I'm not able merely to be myself. I understand I must be willing to lose him, if necessary. I can't have my acknowledgment of who I am along with the image of me which I want with him. To attempt controlling his version of me, so I can "secure his love," I must deny what's going on inside me.

Once I choose my freedom to reveal myself over attempting to manipulate his view of me, I can accept his labels; for it makes sense that he possesses the same right to his inner reactions as I do to mine. The message gets through to me that his judgments aren't wrong for him, nor do they prove me wrong for me. Not "bad," either, are my caring and distress at his opinions, my vehemently proclaiming my chagrin, and my disagreements with his assessments of what I am. I can stop feeling either of us has to be different, no matter what I might prefer of him. His judgments are him, what he is, just as my wanting them a certain way, but not needing their obliging me, are me.

(four months later)

Especially lately, it seems to me, Adam indicates confusion. I wonder if anything is the matter with him. I suppose the thought is born of my anxieties concerning growing older.

(five months later)

After our last go-round my present standpoint, which I've laid out to Adam, is briefly this: I'm no longer choosing to risk expressing vulnerability to him, not until he demonstrates he is able and willing to speak from a standpoint of how he feels, rather than one of informing me about myself and my motivation. If my expressions of negative feelings are interpreted by him as "you shouldn't have" no matter how much I assure him otherwise, it's unrealistic and pointless to think I can communicate with him. End of case.

I've no intention of curtailing my telling him what I like and don't like about what he does. But I'm determined to do so from a position of impersonal energy, to the extent of which I'm capable. I don't want to lose touch with my own feelings of hurt, pain, or whatever, but will honor them privately.

Actually, I'm just as foolish as he is to battle with him over whether or not I'm blaming him. There's no—repeat, no—objective "whether," only his view and mine.

I made one point I wish to make a note of: We feel, in my view, out of our own frames of reference. But we must interpret and judge other persons from theirs. If we don't, we're implying ours is the only correct perspective, hanging in space as universally valid. And we'll never understand our fellow humans.

I'm beginning to feel rather free. It seems to me I've given him every opportunity to move to the standpoint which he says over and over he wants to adopt, that of no-fault/no-blame, no right nor wrong, but only acknowledgment of inner experience. So now I can quit approaching him from a position of even minimal vulnerability in a risk situation (i.e., one involving any negative feelings whatsoever concerning him or any action of his). I of course lose intimacy and, as New Agers put it, "heart connection," but I can't achieve them all by myself. And I plan not to try.

(two weeks later)

I realize the more Adam agrees in calm moments with my frame of reference the more difficult he finds projections onto me of "you're blaming me." So for their protection he requires increasing defensiveness and anger.

(three weeks later)

I told Adam that when he speaks subjectively I no longer feel I must contradict him to preserve my integrity. He's said nothing to take issue with, has let me off the hook.

I remarked, too, I feel we've moved one hundred and eighty degrees. He behaves the way I used to, and I act in the manner he once relied on.

(nine weeks later)

In "cold blood," when Adam isn't feeling defensive, unlike me he thinks documentation equals blaming.

I assured him I'm not asking him to accept my frame of reference, but merely to understand that I act out of mine, not his, and that when I speak it's not for the same reasons which would prompt him were he to articulate my statements. I also once more reminded him that for the last decade I've made the same request: that he credit me with behaving out of my own mindset. When he asked me to cease labeling withdrawal neurotic I changed my viewpoint, but haven't been able to gain the same consideration and respect from him.

He finally conceded that he got my point: His talking "fault" and "blame" automatically assumes that negative feelings shouldn't occur. He also admitted that he indeed is looking for an exact match between stimulus and his emotional response.

I do, however, sense a glimmering of an intuition I even expressed to Adam: If I allow that a schism exists between us and don't try to become or stay understandable to him, I'm free to travel inwardly in my thoughts and emotions wherever or as far as I like. I even can glimpse the freedom I'd gain. Suddenly sacrificing it in order to achieve being comprehended seems like selling my soul to the devil. Yet it's hard to stand alone except for the momentary sop of a partial meeting of minds and hearts.

17. JOURNALISMS: EIGHT

(ten weeks later)

Adam remarked that he's a quiet extrovert and I'm a noisy introvert. I chuckled with appreciation of his perceptiveness.

I told him I think we're both invested in not—repeat, not—getting the feel of what goes on in the other. From my standpoint, if I become too sympathetic I might lose my capacity to express negative feelings. And if he, for his part, sensed basically where I'm coming from, he'd no longer feel attacked and would lose the defense and weapons which that position gives him.

(ten days later)

I asked him to inform our internist he requires more sleep than formerly. He became angry. I followed him into the bedroom to attempt peacemaking. He told me he perceives me as trying to break his spirit, to turn him into someone other than who he is. I think I'm as entitled as he to consider "You're trying to crush my spirit and transform me into a person I'm not."

(three weeks later)

Today I'm feeling resentful of us both, angry, sad. I've lost my spontaneity with Adam. Hard to maintain it even when I'm not negative if I guard against letting it show. I wonder why I'm doing it to myself. I remarked to him very quietly that if we've engaged in a power struggle he's won it. I also told him that this fact to my mind doesn't imply his case is more meritorious than mine, but simply that I'm the one who elected to change so that our relationship ceases to be as adversarial as it had become. He agreed.

These days it's increasingly difficult for me to make any waves in his direction. Only the least little rivulets. No breakers. I don't, I admit, consider I love him more than he does me. Rather, I think, we're playing out cultural roles. He must assert his maleness by "not giving in," and I must evidence my femininity by behaving as the flexible and conciliatory partner.

I'm careful by choice. But I don't like it. It's only that the alternative—angry and pointless arguments—is worse. What if I need to yell and scream even when he's home? I can simply tell him so, go to our bedroom and make as much noise as I please, provided I expel my sounds into a pillow if I use words. He damn well can't call behavior such as that a criticism and an attack. If he does, it's his problem and he'll have to deal with it. There's only so much self-smothering I can manage and still want to stay here.

(two days later)

I find it very difficult to feel or consider myself "in love" when I must watch my style and content of communication. But while "in-loveness" is an extremely enjoyable state I can let it go if necessary. I seem relinquishing of inner demands on him and of expectations. I no longer feel closely linked to him. My sense of our apartness is also an experience of inner freedom. Suddenly it seems even more valuable—meaning inwardly more rewarding—than in-loveness. And to hell with his consequent image of me.

(nine days later)

Adam asked why, if I'm sure of my position, do I mind how he reacts? I answered, in effect: Because being understood is part of connecting, of relationship, so to me an end in itself. He yelled, "Elephant shit!" Me: "Oh, boy." He then announced that I tell him he's crazy, no good and I'm out to destroy his viewpoints. I insisted what I'd said didn't deserve that judgment or that treatment and I wanted an apology within five minutes. I got it.

Adam conceded he feels threatened for inexplicable reasons. They've more to do, he added, with his fearing generally a loss of control as he ages and notices some of his powers slipping. I silently judged his recent charges unfair and irrational. To him I stressed that I wanted us to treat each other as friends as both of us grow older.

(nine days later)

Adam lost the TV program we were watching. I complained. He: "You get so angry about every little thing I don't know what to do." His voice sounded plaintive and helpless. He later apologized, admitted playing victim.

(two months later)

I still feel torn between the side of me who wants to "live" the quarrel and the part who feels I'm thereby a pawn to the situation.

When Adam labels me, if in defense of myself I do anything that smacks of behavior he describes, I've after the fact earned the tag he put on me beforehand. He appears of the opinion that if ever I merit such and such description I always do. Nonsense. If you want me not to deserve your categorizations treat me well.

I'm weary of trying to earn loveability. I'd rather be real and lose him. I choose whenever possible to break through stereotypes of how I'm supposed to behave. I don't wish merely to protest charges I think are abusive; I want to stop them. I'll do what I can to accomplish this aim. And sometimes I won't be loveable, either, but controlling, etc. for reasons of my own, a fact which is okay, too. I hope I can acknowledge when I am.

(two months later)

Adam insists that by documenting with particulars the situations I don't like I'm holding him responsible for my reactions. I rejoinder that I'm simply attempting to give him information about what it is I'm responding to, admittedly always subjectively.

But slowly it has dawned on me that we're both nuts. Who is he that he should never be criticized? And how can I claim I don't, in fact, ever carp or even accuse? It's impossible to express any negative thoughts and emotions without at least implying disapproving or somewhat rejecting judgments. So how can they be forbidden in "fair" fighting?

For me, whether or not his labels fit no longer is the issue. Of course they do. Why shouldn't they? As part of my humanness I've the right to earn them.

(six weeks later)

We agreed that when my issues differ from his he views the discrepancy itself as indication that I'm attacking, controlling, etc.

Adam announced that when I say "I'd prefer you to...," "I'd like it if you...," "I'd appreciate it if you..." I'm telling him what he ought to do. I'm shocked. I thought we'd progressed at least further than his last admission indicates.

18. JOURNALISMS: NINE

(ten months later)

Adam made decisions with the TV cable company without discussing them with me. I confessed that I was furious. He replied, "You control with temper tantrums. That's your style." I took issue with his charge and he apologized.

(four months later)

I asked Adam if he'd hire help with raking our leaves. His reply was no. I wasn't in the least mad, but replied I'm anxious about their blowing on neighbors' lawns. He angrily referred to my "ranting and raving." I insisted he beg my pardon; he did. I confessed my strong impression that for whatever reason he has programmed himself to receive me irately. He conceded: maybe.

(seven weeks later)

Adam falls playing tennis and breaks his leg just below the hip bone. Shortly after insertion of a pin and brace he's transferred to a nursing home. He returns home approximately five weeks later.

(six months later)

I asked Adam why he'd thrown out the directions which came with our new alarm clock. He responded with, "What difference does it make?" I explained why from my standpoint I wanted them. He exclaimed: "Boy!" I countered with, "I could say 'Boy' too." He then began with "Ever since you woke up..." (I'd in fact felt untroubled.) He pressed on and I yelled, "Shut up!," a command I repeated as long as he continued his loud comments. He finally stopped shouting and I warned him to leave me alone, not to goad me.

I felt surprised at myself, and all the rest of the day highly satisfied with the incident.

(five weeks later)

I've several thoughts about Adam's reaction to anger which he confirms. He interprets expressions of irateness as attempts to control him in order to change him. His integrity feels threatened so he digs in his heels.

Also, perhaps because of his fist fights on playgrounds, rage seems to him a fight to the finish, with a winner and loser. So he must return fury in order not to be done in but to survive.

(twenty-one months later)

I think there's a strong possibility I'm a hook for Adam's self-criticisms because he hasn't healed faster from his accident. I also believe I'm a target for his projections of anger at his fall and other infirmities. He's suffered severe nose bleeds, one requiring a two-day hospitalization. He can hang his dark emotions onto me, fight me, not them, as the enemy, and retain his sense of inner unity unconflicted. So he can't afford to learn the attacks on him aren't coming from me, but are his own leveled against himself.

I shared these surmises with Adam and surprisingly he bought into them. He then remarked, "You're a real partner."

I asked him not to underestimate how chronically wounded I find myself all the same. I added I recognize that a lot of the time he feels criticized and the target of anger, though I don't or won't know when or why.

(three weeks later)

I've tried to control with disapproval and irritation. Adam's weapons are feeling criticized and the assumption of innocence. I've a sense that we've been locked unwittingly in a power struggle Adam has won. I've allowed us to curtail my spontaneity almost entirely. I now consider very carefully what subjects to introduce and how to phrase what I say. I try to anticipate all criticisms he might infer and reassure him they're not my message. I monitor my voice to keep it low and quiet. It's all an effort to become a little more understood. I also long to assuage my guilt over his hearing "you should/shouldn't," "you ought/ought not," "you're wrong," when these chidings aren't in my thoughts.

Nonetheless, he tells me in our last go-round that "I feel criticized a lot." I've an unshakeable sense I can't win with him. He's not about to relinquish this stance, in my view, for a perspective more comprehending of where I'm coming from. His predetermination of reaction, as I see it, affords him both innocence and control.

I'm neither feeling nor behaving as I'd wish to in an intimate relationship. I'm guarded now. I refuse, however, to sell out my integrity. If it's important to me to take some stand with him, I will. But I'll watch closely how I word myself.

I feel really withdrawn, a state I don't enjoy. My resentment is my revenge. I'm aware it also hurts me. Nevertheless, right now I'm living it.

(two days later)

I acknowledged to Adam I feel betrayed by my trusting in his good will toward me. I want it sufficient for motivating his willingness to share with me fifty-fifty responsibility for our difficulties. I admitted I understand intellectually his lifelong investment in his innocence. In my view it underlies his "don't make waves" self-rule. And vice versa; what's chicken or egg?

Nevertheless, my heart hurts that his wanting to think well of me, as part of his loving me, can't prove stronger than this stricture.

I added I've a theory: Part of his "don't make waves" admonition to himself is the injunction "Don't be the one who starts a fight." Perhaps he felt unjustly accused of being the culprit by the teacher who interrupted his tussle on the school playground, or by his father when he and his brother skirmished because "You're the older." The latter example seemed to ring a bell.

(ten weeks later)

I now wish to allow myself more spontaneity of expression with Adam, with less concern for his image of me. I perceive his labels as attempts to control me into silence by playing victim and trying to shame me. I strongly desire to relinquish my concern with them. If I've the name I might as well have the game.

(five months later)

Merely my articulation tells Adam, according to his perspective, that I'm accusing him of "causing" my unhappiness. If I accepted my feelings as "just my stuff" I'd resolve them silently to spare him blame—unless, as he's proposed more than once—I enjoy attacking.

19. JOURNALISMS: TEN

(three weeks later)

Adam and I visit our internist because of his increasing difficulty swallowing. We hopefully receive tips to aid improvement.

(three days later)

The appropriateness of labels, categories—mine or his—must no longer matter to me. I want to measure myself—if at all—not by criteria, only by those emotions my actions generate—not in him but in me. I choose as my lodestar my awareness of whatever is within me at the moment of its happening. I'm interested in a self-acceptance as full as possible. And I'll allow my instincts and impulses to devise and direct my course in its own occurring.

My criterion for speaking out will be this: Do I wish to take issue, or, for whatever reason, to articulate? If I regret what I do or say, I'll apologize. I intend to express myself and my feelings whenever and however I choose. I can concede I earn his descriptions of me and still view myself as acceptable. I herewith renounce responsibility for making life pleasant for Adam. I bid farewell to Mrs. Goodwife.

I told him, without anger, I seem once more to be giving birth to myself. I felt both heard and understood by him.

(four days later)

If Adam is entitled to dismiss whatever I say I needn't censor my speech.

~ ~ ~ ~ ~ ~

My wound is his poor image of me. I'll heal it by accepting its actuality, and its belonging to him, not to me, by detaching from my investment in it.

In this moment I'm aware of the gift my hurting gives me: that of freedom, the liberty to be who I am. The hope for, the trying to attain, a positive picture of me in his mind is the carrot hanging in front of the donkey, the ass! It keeps me forever invested in attempting to please him. I'm closer and closer to the point at which whether or not I gain or forfeit his approval becomes for me an irrelevance. My focus is on my authentic living of who I basically am—"am" at least in the moment.

(three weeks later)

We agreed our relationship is becoming sharper, more destructive, is running downhill.. And we concurred in our opinion that our perspectives are increasingly divergent.

(three days later)

I told Adam, and he agreed I might very well be correct, that I think his need of innocence stems not from an attempt to prove virtue but to achieve safety—of some kind.

(five weeks later)

Adam is not the only person entitled to a sense of some degree of innocence. His evidence supporting his own is hardly absolute. As examples, for him "sins" are only of commission (mine) but never of omission (his). His attitude is one of, "What did I do?" "What didn't I do?" doesn't count. Like everyone's, his interpretations are, although scarcely indisputable, entirely to his own advantage: his accusations that my documentations are attempts to hold him responsible for my emotions; his definitions of "I" and "you" statements as opposed to mine; his insistence that he's heard "nothing but," mind you, "heavy control" from me for the past umpteen hours; his ubiquitous use of "always" and "never." His exaggerations and vehemence, to my thinking, indicate how imperative is his need to build an airtight case for himself.

I now believe he can feel safe only if he succeeds in persuading both of us of his innocence. His stance is bolstered by his "don't make waves" modus vivendi.

three days later)

I'm euphoric, at least for now. I'm feeling free not from any connection, but from connectedness itself. Now I'd never choose to return to my former sense of identification with another—in my present case, Adam. And if my situation ever involves me with a second life partner, I intend to guard carefully against accommodation for purposes of a loveable/exemplary image with that person. So I'd make certain I retain my sense of individuality, existential separateness (not separation—at least not necessarily).

~ ~ ~ ~ ~ ~

A couple of thoughts about Adam which now seem very important. That he doesn't "make waves" is at least one of his claims to innocence. I no longer believe he's only or perhaps even mainly attempting to secure his safety. He's an adult and bound to realize his actual survival isn't at stake. Safety from what? Attacks by his inner critic on his self-image, his sense that he's entitled to resist all attempts at changing him.

But I barely care. It's all his stuff. I hope to end my concerns with proving pleasing—to him, perhaps to anyone. I feel buoyant, joyful, free.

(one day later)

It occurs to me that perhaps I can feel more tolerant of Adam's mental slowing down if I'm not having to maintain a picture within myself of a man I'm "in love with."

I've a hunch Adam no longer is much concerned with whether or not I'm very romantically inclined toward him, provided, that is, I allow our relationship to remain intact. He'd also like me from time to time to indicate warm sentiments toward him and share thoughts with him. I'll do so whenever I'm so inclined.

20. JOURNALISMS: ELEVEN

(one week later)

I told Adam and he agreed: He used *Straight Talk* as an excuse with himself to stop backing up—i.e., attempting to be agreeable—when he didn't like what I said to him. By deciding my "Heavy Control" caused our fights he justified his "defensive" broadsiding. As a result of reading the book I tried hard to revise my method and style of communicating. He couldn't hear the changes because not being aware of them suited his purpose: Not accepting that they had occurred justified, for him, his anger (which of course needed no actual justification). His selective interpretations served his investment in establishing (especially with himself) his innocence (of, often, lack of consideration).

The thought occurs to me that the harder I tried to assure him I wasn't holding him responsible for my reactions to him, nor attempting to imply he should be other than who he is, the more mad he became. Of course. I was undermining his "right" to blame me for our quarrel of the moment.

I seem quite self-righteous, don't I, even to my own eyes. I confess I, too, serve my own purposes. I, like he and almost everyone else, justify my reactions and conclusions.

(six weeks later)

Adam announced he felt distanced from me and would like for us to get closer together, if possible. I summarized for him my present state and admitted that what I want now is creation of room for myself to feel disturbed. I don't wish to pretend all is well. I'm in a state of greatest upheaval of any I've experienced since our marriage. We both confessed to feelings of sadness.

(nine weeks later)

Adam told me he thinks his trouble with hearing my perspective about blaming, etc., is a matter of his not wanting to "back up," give up any of his power to me and in so doing unbalance our equality.

(ten days later)

I feel hurt, irate and sad about Adam's and my communications of, roughly, the last decade—more specifically, since we read *Straight Talk* and he decided I'm the one responsible for our difficulties. At this moment I don't want to try being impartial; I wish just to express my thoughts and current emotions.

I feel betrayed. To me, good will consists of wanting to think well of the other. In earlier years I'd assumed I could count on his fair opinion of me, for his sake as well as mine—actually, in behalf of our relationship. Augmenting it seems to me as much in his favor as in mine. I can't understand why he'd want to turn me into villain and himself into victim. I presume he felt threatened, and needed this view of me and our connection as some form of essential protection. But did it never occur to him his judgment of our conflicts is self-righteous? If so, was he content to leave it unrevised? And why?

A few years back he admitted he'd used *Straight Talk* to brand me as the culprit of our quarrels. I thought this realization of his would prove a turning point for us. No such luck. He's continued to come at me in language and terms that are black and white, extreme. True, he no longer talks as much about my speaking in "nothing but heavy control." Now he instead announces that "for the past hour I've heard nothing but blame."

He makes this charge in the face of my declarations of not finding fault inside myself with either of us. Other accusations I find particularly galling are: "You're just trying to justify your reactions"; "You're merely talking about emotion not feeling it"; "I'm hearing no subjectivity at all"; "What is the purpose of this lecture?"; etc.

I no longer trust him with expressions of my vulnerabilities— primarily my fear of losing his love—which in any way pertain to behavior of his. I've ceased to rely on his generosity of spirit to prompt his viewing me in as gentle a light as possible. I've lost faith in even his kindness toward me. At one time I counted on his tolerance in appraising me. And cherished him for it.

His inability, even unwillingness, to hear and attempt

understanding my perspectives from which I speak has eroded seriously my sexual and romantic feelings toward him. How downright stupid of him! How could he not be aware of the advantage to him of my continuing to adore him, as I once did (though I don't think I placed him on a pedestal). Admittedly he's supportive of even negative reactions, and listens well to them provided they don't pertain to his behavior. And he's charitable, too, with his judgments in these impersonal areas. But he's unfair in not allowing me to be in his eyes my own spokesperson about my conscious intentions. In not believing in my sincerity.

(two days later)

I asked Adam whether he considered "I don't like it" and "you shouldn't have done it" two different statements or one and the same. He replied: "It's a hyphenated sentence; they say one thing." I then commented that their constituting completely different declarations containing entirely separate messages is for me the crux of my philosophy of interpersonal relations.

Capsuled versions follow of my reasons for my stand: (1) no thoughts or feelings are crimes; (2) negative judgments are thoughts and therefore allowable as expressions of admittedly only oneself; (3) since no right or wrong exists, neither do grounds for the blaming of "you shouldn't have"; (4) "I don't like it" equals self-accountability; "you shouldn't" presents claims to the outside world that it ought to meet my standards; (5) self-expression is my nature and reclamation of my childhood relinquishment of selfness; (6) not accepting my frame of reference blends two persons into one (you, Adam) and (7) renders communication—i.e., mutual understanding—impossible.

I woke up irritated, then progressed after he left for physical therapy into shouting "I'm free." Meaning: I no longer intend to worry about, or consider myself responsible for, whether or not he hears or feels that comments of mine contain criticism. His emotions stem from his own interpretations based on his personal perspectives.

If I intend expressing disapproval I'll admit it. Yet I've a right to voice negative opinions provided I own them as "my stuff." Who is Adam that he's owed immunity from evoking displeasure? I've felt attacked, too, by him, and survived.

We had a quiet talk. Adam thinks he now accepts that my reasons for talking are different from his, and that he'd assumed they were the same.

We shall see. Mainly I feel liberated from trying to achieve and maintain a good image with him. I've arrived at this point before, I realize, but my hope of being understood by him has been slow to corrode. Actually, I'm freer to be myself without it. The down side of this fact is my sense of loneliness. But all has its price.

(nine days later)

In Adam's view I'm not entitled to judgments of him, his behavior, which are critical. I should couch my appraisals of him to myself in ways which remove all actual disapproval, even that which I fully personalize. "Negative" responses should consist only of emotion, not assessment, especially in any reactions I voice to him.

My standpoint is this: All I need communicate to him if he misunderstands me is my conscious intention. What he does with such a statement, judgmentally or emotionally, is up to him.

(seven months later)

Considering mere acknowledgment of emotion to be an attack requires acceptance of the premise that not all feelings are permissible. I think they are.

Adam agrees his viewpoint has been: Painful emotions are the fault of the person experiencing them. They evidence his or her failure to deal with life appropriately. By not conceding the blame for mine should fall on me, I'm implying it belongs to him. In this implication lies my "attack."

But if truly "no feeling crimes" exist, what could be blameable? And if psychic pain is simply an inner happening that's part of life, neither its source nor its effect is culpable.

Adam claims he wants to shift his perspective to one which espouses a premise of "no fault, no blame."

(six months later)

Adam declared that feeling criticized is only a momentary reaction which doesn't hurt him permanently. But his protest has been "I'm attacked for who I am," a serious violation of his personhood. I added that my irritations are also fleeting.

(six months later)

I voice negative emotions—yes, he's right—but not about who he is; rather, in reaction to his specific behaviors of the instant. I consider the difference a telling distinction to make.

When he objects to my expressiveness he gives me a case just as

199

valid as his for considering "I'm criticized for who I am." If this realization occurs to him he doesn't mention it.

In my view "I feel criticized..." expresses emotion; "...for who I am" constitutes interpretation.

(four months later)

When chasing a falling lightbulb in the kitchen Adam crashes to the floor. He breaks his upper leg just below his unimpaired hip. I sleep on a couch in his room at the hospital until he returns home three weeks later. We hire nursing help for him.

(two months later)

Today I realize the strength of my inner sense that I've changed much. I no longer am content to curry favor, but am far more interested in becoming who I am, often by expressing it. My reasons, I think, are mainly two:

1. Investment in one's effect on another person inevitably and invariably throws one at his mercy. This somebody has his own program to achieve, his axe to grind. No winning is possible on one's personal terms when the issue is the other's agenda. To triumph inside his head requires the sacrifice of one's own interests and integrity.

2. I'm probably running out of time for attaining and firming up further self-realization, self-actualizing.

But, ah, what a sense of empowerment comes with self-focus.

21. JOURNALISMS: TWELVE

(two weeks later)

Adam and I discussed his current emotional state, or lack of it. He stated he's decided, he thinks, that to survive he needs to stay in his head, not in his feelings. I argued that I believe the reverse. But I conceded that he, of course, is the only person who can choose his path.

A thought occurs to me. Since his fall and fracture he's been considerably incontinent. In addition, his esophagal action is at times giving him trouble swallowing. And we both have admitted his cognitive functions have slowed, according to Adam ever since his fall five years ago. I agree with his assessment.

I now wonder if it isn't possible that the trauma of his fractures and operations affected his brain? But so what, if so? It's still important for everyone to implement enlivening intellectual activity. Why should we not purposefully exercise emotions also by pursuing awareness of feelings in the moment? He claims he wishes to rediscover his.

Our former relationship seems history.

(two weeks later)

Adam declared he needs an optimistic attitude to recover from his fall. He therefore doesn't choose to allow himself darker emotions.

~ ~ ~ ~ ~ ~

I've warned him that for the maintenance of my self-respect I intend to continue complaining when I decide I'm not being treated considerately. Like him, I deserve to be counted as a person.

Our relationship has changed in every respect in recent years. I grieve and mourn the loss of the past we shared. I do so despite my progress, partly resulting from my frustrations at times with our connectings, in permitting myself to become who I am today. I'm accepting the fact that I'm alone. Our intimacy, especially on the emotional level, has diminished and to some extent is nonexistent.

But an advantage of my present state is this: I don't consider I owe him—I repeat "owe"—any predecided attitude or feeling. I feel free of emotional and intellectual obligation toward others and even toward him. And that step I can say sincerely is a biggy.

I do think he's entitled to my behaving decently and lending him, while I preserve my honesty, my full encouragement of every kind which I can manage. I'll never forget, I hope, his support of all my endeavors and projects.

I'm prepared for his detaching from me emotionally whenever he's threatened with an upsetting involvement which the state of my own health might cause him.

Somehow I feel mostly resigned, accepting of my situation and who he is today. I still have me.

(three days later)

We'd left the surgeon's office after Adam's check-up visit. Looking backward at me he stumbled a bit. I felt as rageful as I always do when he nearly or actually tumbles. Once home, I sermonized to him about the need for both our sakes of his taking care of himself. I announced to him that, like him, I must survive. I can't endure another period resembling the past three months. Next time I won't stay at the hospital. I found sleeping there every night on a narrow couch for twenty-one days exhausting. And when he's discharged he'll at least temporarily have to enter a rehab center.

The patriarchy postulates it's okay for him to give first priority to his own survival. But I, being woman and wife, lack the right to equalize my welfare with his. I must service him regardless of cost to myself. No. I won't do it. I'm finding it hard to stand against my Inner Patriarch. Nevertheless, once Adam is ambulatory I'm ready to set up my life more to my liking.

Adam's choice of blocking his feelings and thereby thwarting our intimacy has given me a gift. It's freed me to reclaim my own existence. I hope I'm a decent, compassionate human being. But I find myself considerably unburdened of expectations and claims on myself—those of others and my own—which I don't choose to honor. I also feel relieved to quite an extent of my sense of obligation to take care of him according to his preferences at my own expense. Yet I can put up with a lot of demands on my energies and time as long as I can manage minutes and hours for myself.

(five days later)

I admitted to Adam I'm more volatile emotionally than before he retreated from his feelings. I intuit I'm compensating for the void, the vacuum, of emotional diminishment between us. In other words, I'm attempting to live feelings for us both.

I confessed to him he seems a stranger to me now; I don't know him. He admitted he's changed, and not to his liking. I'd never have predicted he'd choose his present path. I'm deeply disappointed. In my opinion he ignored an opportunity and challenge to grow in broadening his field of, and capacity for, emotional experience. His blandness, his monotonal feeling reactions, his inability to spark or be sparked, frankly speaking, bore me.

(one day later)

Adam did express some of his emotions, and with tears in his eyes. He revealed that formerly he felt young; now he feels old. He's lost so much weight that his skin sags. He worked hard for five years to recover from his first fall and now all his effort seems in vain. Hardest part of his present life is his inability to sleep comfortably without back pain.

That night when I gave him a Tylenol PM he gagged and couldn't keep it down. The last three months, he told me, have proved to be the worst of his life.

Since that confession I've felt tenderly and fully loving. But I don't want to fall back, because of my present emotional state, into the trap of becoming Mrs. Goodwife.

(one week later)

In view of Adam's increasing difficulties with swallowing we visit a gastroenterologist. His diagnosis: Adam isn't a candidate for surgery, but must eat "mush" for the rest of his life.

(two days later)

I realize that in part I feel I betray Adam by permitting who I am to change. I've ceased to be the person he bargained for when he married me. In our present circumstances I resent his physical dependence on me because it deprives him of options: He's stuck with having me around. If he could make it alone he could leave if who I've become doesn't please or satisfy him. Not so now.

But here's a consoling thought: He's entitled not to love me, and to the self-protection of withdrawal. So he's not powerless. Is his remoteness these days resulting in part from a process of detaching from me?

(five days later)

We had quite a set-to. It began with my spouting my philosophy about the crucialness of experiencing one's feelings. He announced I don't know him, don't care about him, and tell him what to do. I replied I've a right to fight for the vitality of our relationship by expressing my own beliefs. If he's not willing to concede the point, I'm now as capable as he of checking out on our intimacy. He became tearful and voiced the fear of losing me. I agreed my further inner withdrawal from him is a real possibility since contact requires emotional circuity.

I didn't anticipate what followed: a declaration that his greatest loss from his fall and esophagal problem is his absence of feeling. He continued: He really worked hard to arrive where he was before his accident and surgery; he doesn't want to die inwardly; he seems to himself muted, vanilla. He doesn't know how to fill his inner vacantness.

I observed that he was right then in touch with his feelings, they do exist, but I conceded I've the image of a bomb ripping through a shelter and leaving a gaping hole. He sounds in the throes of post-traumatic stress disorder and my only recommendations are faith and patience.

I admitted I'd decided in recent months that his retreat from emotion was more of a conscious decision than I now consider it is.

I've never loved him more than during his outpouring. We both acknowledge how fully we feel out of control of our future lives.

22. JOURNALISMS: THIRTEEN

(three weeks later)

Adam remarked he's more concerned with the restrictions on his walking than on his eating. I expressed irritation: He's giving no thought to the deprivation to me resulting from his inability to dine in restaurants. Eating out, I've told him often, is one of my joys. I announced I feel not counted, a nonentity to him. It's I who'd insisted we again try sleeping in the same room, only to be told he needed the entire bed to thrash in. Come on; with a broken hip?. He apologized, stating he's so worried about his progress that he's self-centered.

These days I'm accepting Adam as my job, unfortunately not my joy. Those years when our relationship had vitality for me have evaporated. He's monosyllabic, flat, slow in his replies I must dig for. And obviously depressed. Any pleasure our joint company gives me is a bonanza.

My actual expectations of him are minimal. I still intend, however, to speak my reactions to behavior of his I find slighting, and any others I care to express. With emotion. I grant myself the right to exist without feeling smothered. He can respond however he pleases.

(one day later)

My feelings are hurt that the rewards of our partnership can't rescue him from despondency. He tells me I'm central to his existence, but I'm not, certainly not these days. His focus is almost wholly on his rate of recovering walking ability, and the fact, he hopes, of its continuing to happen.

Harder to take, I'm undergoing frustration and disempowerment. I've no more suggestions to offer him, and he doesn't improve. I ask myself without finding an answer if my "being myself" hurts or helps his situation. I wonder if I'm toxic to him. My Inner Patriarch lists the virtues I should be demonstrating—tolerance, acceptance, empathy, etc.—none of which match my present attitudes and emotions (with the exception of, at moments, some empathy). I'm caught in a constant state of guilt whenever I'm not "lovely" to him, one I resent enduring.

I don't know what to do for him, or what I "should" do. I told him I'm throwing back at him all responsibility for his improvement. Not because I don't care about him, but because I'm ignorant of how I "ought" to be for his benefit. In addition to previous possibilities for him I've proposed specific tapes and books. I'm sunk within the "cloud of unknowing," suspecting that answers, especially since they concern another person, won't be forthcoming.

With fear and trepidation I'll stick with "being myself," at least for now.

~ ~ ~ ~ ~ ~

I realize that Adam's focus on himself is a result of his depression. That fact, however, doesn't neutralize my reaction to his "not counting" me.

I also told Adam I'm now considering he, not I, is responsible for deciding and expressing how I harm or can assist him. I asked him whether my telling him, as I frequently have the past few months, "I want a response, a reaction," hurts, helps or is neutral in its effect on him. He replied: the last. I'm rather relieved.

(two weeks later)

Adam asked when we might cancel having nursing aides come, if I myself would prefer letting them go. I was irate. At least a dozen times I've described how unpleasant I find the nearly constant presences in my home of other women, the invasion of my space, the never-ending sound of TV, etc. I charged that when he can't remember what I've emphasized over and over as vital to me I feel I don't matter to him.

Last night I told Adam as we got into bed that I felt really lonesome. He was sweet. We had a gentle talk lying down, he saying he hoped to regain his feelings. He stated quietly, "I love you very much." I suggested that the statement contradicted his declaration of being out of touch with his emotions. He admitted that what he actually meant is "I love you somewhat." My calm reaction is: "That's the way it is."

Often in recent weeks the thought has come to me: "It's over," meaning our past relationship; certainly at least for now. To quite an extent I accepted this fact some time ago. I grieve my loss of former delights.

As for my current reactions to it all: considerable detachment; a realization that what-is in fact is, and what will be will be. Most of my eggs are by no means placed in the basket of our connectedness; far fewer than formerly. Assuming he recovers his emotional capacities, I strongly suspect I'll never again fully trust him not to withdraw them when stressed by circumstances either he or I present him with.

My primary investment appears to be in self-search writing in my journal. I surprise myself with how often my mood proves to be untroubled and buoyant.

(one month later)

Adam symbolizes himself as a wild horse. Today I envision him as a horse wearing blinders. The healing, if it occurs, can come only from, and through, him. At present he focuses singly on increasing his mobility, and on blocking awareness of all else. He seems to view any interruption of his single-mindedness as a distraction from his progress down the path of bettering his walking.

He's fearful of letting in his darker feelings: fear, rage, resentment, guilt, etc. He admits he's frightened of disintegrating, nonsurvival. I spoke passionately of the freedom and joy resulting from no longer having—repeat, having—to continue living.

(one month later)

I admitted earlier that Adam hurt my feelings with his wishing to sleep alone in our double bed. Today I mentioned to him my belief that at that time he was invested in playing the role of invalid. He agreed. He also offered that he thought his attitude then was "silly." I added, "rejecting."

(one week later)

We've in my view misinterpreted his emotions as attitudes. His pessimism, frustration, etc., are the intellectual representations of his blacker feelings to which he's unaccustomed. He could and did, I think, find them threatening but less so when considered to be thoughts, which appear more containable than emotions.

Until now he has allowed himself and experienced mostly cheerful feelings. But his present health situation has broken through his defenses and presented him with unhappy but entirely appropriate emotions. His lifelong self-sufficiency and supportiveness of others also has given way, these to dependency and self-centeredness.

His crisis has caused him to enlarge emotionally, stretch his capacity for encountering aspects of himself previously more or less buried. He's undergoing, to me, a painful but eventually rewarding inner-growth experience. I assured him he deserves allowing himself pride in his capacity to respond to "contingency" not as a Polly Anna but as an alive, honest human being.

23. JOURNALISMS: FOURTEEN

(two weeks later)

Adam and I talk about his choices for himself: re-engagement in life or slipping gently on into old age and death. I've assured him that for my sake I want him here but it's his own wishes which must prevail.

(one month later)

I find myself in a depressed and grieving mode. I mourn: the loss of all that Adam's and my relationship once was; the end of partnered sex; my disappearing youngness; diminishment of my health; my death approaching at some point in the future; the disagreeable chores and obligations of my days; and perhaps especially the loss of time for writing.

Lament the whole of it, I counsel myself, but let it go; allow all of it simply to drift off from me. Give up not only expectations but each and every criteria of judging us or anything. Exist in and for the present moment only.

Circumstances and my life process have brought me to this hour and situation. As a person wishing to behave with decency I elect to stay in it. My choice, then, is to be here now no matter how reluctantly, right where I am. And my first job is to carve into my day as much writing time as I can manage.

My second is to cultivate more empathy toward Adam. None of my losses is his fault. Why not contribute to his happiness as much as I'm genuinely able to? I want to give myself the gift of feeling I'm "counting him," treating him with a consideration that includes warmness.

(three weeks later)

Adam is due for his annual physical exam. I've written to our internist stating my reasons for thinking Adam may be suffering from

209

Parkinson's. I've been reading about the disease. Among symptoms evident in him is his fixed stare, now fairly obvious.

How honest can I be with Adam regarding my reactions to and with him? Snarling as I've been off and on today, I'm making both of us miserable. Can I express myself in a mild tone of voice without going bonkers from our blandness? I confess I've a need to stir us up so I can feel I'm still alive. And he's asked me to challenge and stimulate him.

He claims he's trying not to make waves with me because he worries about my health and is fearful of riling me up. So he makes me responsible for his emotional blocking. He transforms it into a favor to me! I protested. I assured him his attempting to placate me is harder on my heart than any amount of anger he might ventilate. I reminded him that atrial fibrillation and mitral valve prolapse have accompanied me at least since my early twenties. And I'm still here.

I admit I hate living with the person he's become. Can I, will I, say it? I hate him. At least at times. I'm with him now not because of my feelings for him, but for my self-respect. I want to behave like a worthwhile human being.

He's just undergone a gagging episode with breakfast. I felt compassion.

(three days later)

Adam voiced a realization that one motive, at least, for his blocking of his feelings is this: He'd rather be judged inwardly dead than, as he views himself now, stupid and incompetent, a partial person only. A man who can't control even his urinary and bowel functioning. I commented that he's talking about his own self-image projected onto others. He agreed.

I also suggested that it's more frightening to consider himself the victim of circumstances than to brand himself deficient; he's less in charge if he's ever fully subject to contingency. The existential problem is, nonetheless, that in fact he isn't master of his own destiny; none of us is; we die.

~ ~ ~ ~ ~ ~

I use fury to escape fear. To feel overwhelmed is to throw in the towel. Rage not only energizes me; it sends me this message: "I dislike this situation enough to find a solution to it."

I do enjoy becoming, but not remaining, angry.

~ ~ ~ ~ ~ ~

In reaction to little incidents I told Adam that in my opinion he's subjecting me to passive aggression. He concurred and even added that his operating premise of "don't make waves" does indeed lead there as his only outlet.

I'm not irritated by having to do what Adam can't. What gets to me is his making work for me in ways which seem, at least to me, avoidable. So I let fly at moments when holding in feels inviting of inner explosion. But I'll try to be as composed as possible.

If I accept him without expectations I must afford myself the same leniency, generosity. Like him, I'm a person and deserve forbearance as much as he does.

~ ~ ~ ~ ~ ~

Together we visit our internist. He confirms that in all probability Adam has Parkinson's.

(one day later)

I feel loving, protective, even maternal toward Adam. I'll strive for and predict an increase in my tolerance of his behavior I'm not fond of.

(two weeks later)

Adam has reacted to our doctor's diagnosis optimistically. He decided his prescribed medication would alleviate his symptoms. But our physician warned me that Adam's physical mechanism is giving out and he'll suffer a gradual decline. I've said nothing to Adam about this prognosis.

In particular lately I feel myself the target of passive aggression from him: pokes in bed, candy wrappers on the floor, the portable phone placed elsewhere than on its cradle, Polident left in the sink where it sticks when it dries. He tracks mud on the carpet. Now I discover on the bathroom rug a pile of feces onto which he'd dropped his trousers. They were smeared top and bottom.

When I questioned Adam he confessed he doesn't wish me at this time to be expressive. He stated that I'm hurting his self-image; he feels criticized many times a day and infers "I can't do anything right." He claimed I'm informing him how he should run his life. But, he added, he wants us to continue talks about his psyche, PTSD, depression.

I reminded him I'd asked many times if he'd prefer me to rein in. And I assured him I wouldn't for any prize in the world willingly hurt him, especially during these difficult days for him. I asked for and received his forgiveness.

So why have I all along voiced my feelings, thoughts, even advice? I've decided his emotional flatness kept him well defended against undue upset. My spontaneity allowed me outlet and self-exploration. It supported my feeling partially connected to him emotionally. It also relieved the atmosphere of our home from total flatness. Additionally, I'd hoped to jostle him into feeling-type responses.

He obviously can't cope now with more than his physical and psychological difficulties. I'm accepting this fact as an absolute and intend always to deal with him ever so guardedly. Today my outlook about our present status is matter-of-fact: one further step onward from all that was. I'm not yet grieving over the death of (at least for me) our intimacy. Perhaps I've discharged already much of my sorrow. In any case, Adam now seems to me to be my charge and job.

He still elects to talk exploringly. He fully deserves support and recompense for all he's given to me. In addition, I feel much tender compassion for him. I want and resolve to be as helpful to him as possible.

But I'd like to think of a spot where, if and when I need to, I can scream and howl.

I tell Adam I'm aware I'm slipping back into indulging my expressiveness with considerable intensity. I voice guilty feelings about this behavior. I cry as I speak. He replies he's now handling my articulations well. I state I can almost exclusively manage to conduct myself pleasantly, but if I do, I'll end all sense of intimacy with him. I can retain it by exploring myself aloud, even if he responds only minimally.

The issue of his reactions to me is one he must deal with himself. I'll do my best to consider all he's contending with, monitor and discipline myself accordingly. Yet if I'm to feel we're still partners I can bottle up only to the point of not smothering my output. He must choose which course he wants me to follow. He replied strongly that he wishes me to speak out, not just for my sake but his as well: Connection with me is important to him. Again, I'll attempt to achieve the Buddhist "Middle Way," compassionate toward us both.

24. JOURNALISMS: FIFTEEN

(five weeks later)

Despite an increase in aspirating, Adam is not allowing time between bites. For four days I sat at the table as he ate, prompting him to count to three, as our doctor advised, between each mouthful. Suddenly I screamed, "I won't do this." I determined, as I made clear to him, to turn over to him everything—and I do mean everything—he can do for himself. I announced I'll no longer take initiative for attempting to elicit responses from him, emotional or otherwise, encouraging him to use the computer, suggesting stimulating activities, etc. I'm available for all of the above, but only at his instigation. If he wants or needs other help I'll try to oblige if the request seems to me reasonable, but he must ask for my assistance. With my hovering, I realize, I've attempted to maintain a form of contact when other kinds of connection—emotional, intellectual—seem quite limited. The time has arrived to let go of this effort to bond, crippling to both of us.

While I napped he fell off a footstool. Fortunately the only damage was a cut to his arm. What if he gets to the point of needing full-time help and prefers to stay here, rather than enter some kind of facility? I plan to rent a place for me and this computer where for a while I can escape the nursing aides. I won't tolerate without respite a life in their presences.

(two weeks later)

I told Adam I've felt manipulated for roughly one year by his threat of falling if I don't service him. He agreed that he does in fact subject me to this fear of his, but implied it results entirely from the actual situation. I haven't yet devised a way of counteracting this message my conscience sends me: If he tumbles the fault might lie with my not having taken proper care of him. The possibility of such a situation holds me hostage.

(two weeks later)

Adam suffers a profuse nosebleed. I transport him to a nearby hospital by ambulance.

(three weeks later)

Adam aspirates blood.

(one week later)

I assure Adam I never mind unavoidable chores and activities. But those resulting from his carelessness and thoughtlessness gall me. I must remind him to take his pills, goad him to bathe, pick up his mess from the kitchen table. He forgets to swallow between bites and sips. I suspect he's indulging in passive aggression. In any case, playing nursemaid/mother saps my time and energy. Worse, it keeps him the main focus inside my head so that my thoughts are pushed aside.

I've also accepted—again—that in many ways he's become an old man. His incontinence is now virtually total. In any case, I must view him as the patient, mine, and detach as much as I'm able from emotional involvement in his behavior or lack of it. I need to take him as my job. My new mantra, figuratively speaking, is "let go of it." I want not to be nasty to him; he's sweet and perhaps can do no better than his present functionings. Whatever the case, it's beside the point of results to me. Mainly I mustn't waste my time and energies struggling to change that which I don't control: him. For my own sake let me settle for Adam as he is. Yes, I can protest if I wish, but I hope I expend as little of myself as possible doing so. Amen. For today. And now I actually feel loving toward him.

(ten days later)

I'm angry. I feel that in some ways Adam betrayed me. He has supported me always, for which I've thanked him innumerable times, when he doesn't feel threatened in some fashion. Yet if the situation has carried with it connotations unpleasant for him, he's ducked out of involvement with it and me. As examples:

I went to our internist fearing cancer. I asked Adam if he wished me to call in my test results to him as soon as I received them. (They fortunately were negative.) His response was, "You want me to hang by the phone for two hours?" After I came home he apologized.

My sole TIA landed us in the hospital's emergency room. Adam shortly announced, "I'd like to go home." Our insurance coverage included the cost of a private room. We'd chosen it so we could be there for an ailing one of us.

Today I quietly tell him that his self-absorption when we returned from his second hospital stay seemed particularly exemplified by two happenings: his banishing me from our bed until I insisted on returning there; and his "I'm afraid I can't do anything about your birthday." This last despite my informing him earlier I'd like a ring for my middle finger (which I volunteered to shop for). That, or any of the videos I'd marked in the catalog lying near him. He never made a selection.

Yet he does have much to contend with. And his capacities for emotion and meaningful participation in any confrontation are now decidedly limited. Why attack him further?

~ ~ ~ ~ ~ ~

Were I to find myself alone once more I wouldn't choose to fall in love again, and certainly not to marry. As one male friend expressed it, "It's having to accommodate that's the stopper." But I entertain some feelings of guilt about this attitude. They take the form of such thoughts as these: "One must stay open to life, vulnerable to whatever happens if one isn't to lose one's feelings. So I should allow my life's process to unfold as it will."

But I've a right to let myself decide: "I've had romance. For me intense and sexual involvement with another human being belongs to a phase of my existence that has passed. I want to move on. A person 'can't serve two masters.'" Certainly I long to remain passionately enmeshed in living. I speak of focusing the object of my caring and commitment elsewhere than with another human being. I want to devote myself fully and without distraction to writing as self-exploration. And to meditation? Of one kind or another? An unequivocal "of course."

Let me follow my bent, my star, of my life's period unfolding in the moment. Without paying homage to shoulds.

~ ~ ~ ~ ~ ~

Already I can sense a further pullback emotionally from Adam. Do I still hope to challenge him, change him? Come on!

I'll strive to do the best I can by him in current circumstances.

(six days later)

We search to replace my car wrecked by another's "driver inattention." A breeze topples Adam in an auto parking lot.

(ten days later)

Adam begins eleven hours of aspiration.

(three days later)

Irritations with Adam accumulated and I became testy. In apologizing I described my experience of my life today: Frustration at almost no time to write intensified by my sense that time may be running out for me; it in turn underscored by fear of possible increase in my heart difficulties; no compensatory intimacy with him; the majority of my waking hours spent in performing the kind of chores and servicing (housework and nursing) that run counter to my innate inclinations.

Each of us admitted to not liking very much the person the other had become. We agreed, though, that loyalty to our joint history, our mutual love, and circumstances mostly not of our creating bind us together now and for the future. He admitted he somewhat "blows off" my expressions of disturbance: a relief to me. I described my sense of autonomy ever-growing in the months since his second fall. I told him I cherish it and will preserve it.

But I confessed I've also undergone a lessening of trust in the reliability of another's emotional commitment to me: a sort of loss of innocence. I assured him, however, that I'm available for emotional connection if and whenever he is.

25. JOURNALISMS: SIXTEEN

(two weeks later)

Adam loses his balance and falls in our entrance hall. A male neighbor helps get him into my car for taking him to our internist. On arrival home Adam suffers a TIA.

(three days later)

Adam falls over the bed's guard rail and lands on the floor. I take him by ambulance to the nearest hospital. He receives four stitches for a cut to his upper lip, a bandage on his right arm and a tetanus shot.

~ ~ ~ ~ ~ ~

(one month later)

I'm trying not to dwell on the prospect of, in all probability, having to live with other women in the house full-time as long as he's here at home.

I must concede that a nasty little part of me is willing to upset him and possibly worsen his condition in order to hasten his death. There. I've written it.

(one day later)

Driving home from the grocery store I begin to cry. I identify with Adam's distress over being able no longer to put weight on his legs. Mobility always has loomed importantly to him and to be deprived of it is bound to prove devastating. I feel loving, tender and empathic.

(three months later)

This morning when Adam's caretaker had driven him to physical therapy I lay on the bed sobbing and screaming: in grief for the loss of the rest of my life. My black side is out. My despair is essentially unrelated to Adam. I mourn the nonexistence of (1) any reasonable degree of time for myself, and (2) solitude. Having someone else living with us is becoming more and more impossible for me. I feel disrupted, encased, imprisoned, stifled, buried by my present-day life with its unforeseeable end, one very possibly not occurring until after I die. Worn out by nothingness.

The present source of my distress is the circumstances of my life: the extra work involved in having another person living with us twenty-four hours a day; the disruption of my preferred methods of operating in our house; the lack of quiet time to myself. This third persons impose on me mostly through no fault of theirs.

I can't stash Adam away in a nursing home. At least not today. He deserves to be treated kindly, to live, even, when he's valiantly concerned with his physical recovery.

I wonder if at some level I'm trying to undermine his motivation to survive. I need to confess the possibility here. I also, completely on the other hand, want to spur him into vitality in counteraction to his blandness.

I give up on how I affect him. His issues now must be solely his. For meaner or gentler I do my best. And I withdraw. But I do envy him his plentitude of time, which from my standpoint he wastes.

(three weeks later)

I'm turning over to Adam control of his behavior, including attuneness to and articulation of his feelings. When I try to elicit them, because he frequently has asked me to, I receive only "I think" statements. I'm evoking passive resistance in him and in me a sense of futility. I really know now I must detach from any involvement not invited by him with his health or inner life; that is, if our relationship is not to become increasingly antagonistic.

What we had is gone. The man I was in love with has virtually disappeared. It may be he'll come and go a bit. I'm now on my own. I'll take care of Adam as considerately as I'm able. I'm also ready to respond to any of his initiatives. Otherwise, that's it. I've had it; and I've been had. I'm weary and ready to resign all vestiges of role as his savior.

(one week later)

I chronically wake up angry with Adam. Not at him because he has Parkinson's and not mainly at the current circumstances of our lives. I'm upset at his continuing to block his emotions. I'm especially perturbed by his lack of zest for living. He pursues none of the interests he claims, but mostly just sits and dozes. I'm put out with him when he seemingly makes no attempt at processing what I say sufficiently to draw any reasonable conclusion. Instead, he merely asks me indirectly to repeat. He replies to every question I ask him by only posing another. I'm mad because he does nothing to augment his mental acuity. I'm especially frustrated when he falls asleep in the middle of a conversation with me, half denying he's done so.

I feel disrespectful of his talking out both sides of his mouth concerning the path he wishes to travel from now on. He claims he longs to re-engage with life, yet takes no steps to increase his inward or outward involvement. He refuses adherence to either course, detachment or participation, preferring to straddle the commitment fence. His passivity gets under my skin; he waits for his emotions, his enthusiasms, to enter the house and claim him.

I think I've become more unaccepting of him as-is ever since his MRI showed no brain damage worse than mine. Neither of us any longer can use head-trauma as an excuse for him. Nevertheless, I concede he's wounded both physically and by his initial PTSD which followed his second hip breakage.

Mostly, I'm impatient with his lack of awareness, his unwillingness to admit, that his actions belie he wants to live fully. He seems to me not to deal honestly with either of us when he makes this claim which appears to me to be false.

There. I feel better.

But I do wish my emotions about him were at least more neutral, if not more positive. So what can I do about myself? At least for the moment simply admit who I am, obviously not a very tolerant person, and befriend my own reactions as "my stuff."

In my behalf: At times, and even when I'm not with him, my compassion for him can run strong. As does my love, these days unfortunately rather momentarily.

(two days later)

A strong reason why I'm angry with Adam is that he no longer is a man I can feel in love with. And a prominent part of me revels in inner romantic mood and experience. One cause of my cooling toward him is that he doesn't appear even internally involved erotically with me. Another contributing factor: his mental slowness. I could tolerate it, however, were I not turned off by the dearth in his present makeup of compelling interests, his overall lack of psychological vigor. Is he mentally failing, or chiefly lazy in the head? In either case I live with results, not causes.

Why don't I try focusing more pointedly on the advantage to me in the diminishment of my former emotions toward him? It frees me of my Inner Patriarch's craving to please him, prove myself feminine to him and, above all, loveable to him. I frankly no longer care whether or not he cherishes me, and don't need him to. As I remarked earlier, "Man (using the generic term) cannot serve two masters." And now I'm at liberty to foster my writing and my own self.

I do, though, long to behave kindly toward him for the sake of my own self-esteem. And if inside my head and in my behavior toward him I get off his case, perhaps more gentleness with him, affection for him, will follow. As for compassion, it often eludes me and I don't want to bully myself by attempting to force any of my emotions.

So I'll fumble along. And as the monarch in *The King and I* put it, I'll "do my best for one more day."

(four months later)

Adam admits he hasn't found me as loveable in the last few years as he did earlier. I feel hurt and angry. It seems to me I deserve more from him, considering my life since his second hip operation has been devoted in large measure to him. I assumed the reason for his "cooling" is that I'm more harsh than formerly. But, no. He explains it's my current lack of buoyancy and joyfulness that somewhat puts him off.

In response, I rhapsodize about my dark side, its enlargements of me and my self-awareness, its contributions to my inner experiencing. I know as I speak to him I wouldn't give up my blackness, its descents on me, for anything, anyone. His unvoiced reaction is his business, and probably the price I must pay for allowing my demons to take me over at times.

At any point I could die. In my time remaining my primary concern must be my evolving, no matter the path it takes, one unknown to me in this present. So be it.

(one month later)

I've become in the last two years focused more than ever on my self-awareness and on the self-expression conveying emotions which prompts it.

Who I am, inwardly and articulated, is all I have left that's central to my life. To deny it, bury it, is to give in to the death of any meaningful existence for me.

And the increase in my autonomy is perhaps worth the cost of required relinquishments. I know this much: I've no wish or will to revert to any patriarchal aspects of my former feelings and functions. If Adam would like me to reclaim them he's out of luck.

I no longer will hold myself responsible for whether or not he talks to me.

(seven weeks later)

I plan speaking out as I please, but intend to cancel my emotional involvement in results with him.

I've dropped my investment in these other considerations: Whether or not he takes care not to fall, eats enough, swallows twice between bites, remembers to exercise his walking, enters into any quickening mental activities.

One of my motivations for this most recent letting go is: Either he doesn't comprehend, or he doesn't remember, my remarks no matter how crucial I, at least, consider them. I don't know if he's unable to tune in, or balks at speaking when he's uncomfortable with our dialogue. It doesn't matter which. I live with his behavior (or lack of it), not his reasons for it, known or even to him unknown.

Yesterday I felt unburdened, light, untroubled, loving and empathic towards him. I realize unless I disgorge myself of my negativities—yes, often aloud to him—I'm stuck in them and can't move on.

Today he admits he thinks he may not live much longer. I agree. He's increasingly short of breath and often coughs dryly.

I will take care of him here as long as possible. I view him as my ward.

In part, I hope he dies, for his sake and my own. Yet I'm aware I'd miss him mightily were he to leave my life.

(one week later)

Adam's breathing becomes labored. His nurse and I drive him to our doctor's office, where he recovers.

26. JOURNALISMS: SEVENTEEN

(six weeks later)

Adam's feet swell. Again, his nurse and I take him to our internist.

(two days later)

Adam refuses to talk when I question him about what he wants to eat, etc., only shakes his head for yes or no. I finally ask him if these days he wants a personal relationship with me. He replies no. So, I continue, does he still wish to celebrate our wedding anniversary in July? Again, no. He concedes he's showing he's angry, but doesn't know why. His nurse and I take him for his appointment with his neurologist. He has no idea what year it is; first guesses 1980, then 1990, what "the millenium" refers to or where he is. The doctor informs me he considers Adam transitional between stages three and terminal four, a diagnosis our internist confirms. To him I admit I don't know how much longer I can care physically for Adam. He named two facilities where he sees patients. In one, he's medical director.

Today I finalize for myself that I shouldn't pull Adam up any more. When I try to my back is increasingly painful. I'm remembering I count as well as he. And if I injure my body into incapacity I'm no use to either of us.

Having made the decision that Adam probably must go to a nursing facility, I'm aware of conflicting emotions. Part of me feels guilty for "abandoning him"; another side exultantly thinks "I'll get my life back."

(one day later)

Sometimes I'm short with Adam so he'll not mind too much moving into a nursing facility. I try not to call him unpleasant names but I do apply them out loud to specific behavior of his. I find myself wishing he'd die so I can reclaim my own existence. I resent circumstances more than I inwardly fume at the man himself, but my acidity of emotion spills over into objections to his actions. Why doesn't he insist on moving into a care-taking home? Why not spare me the onus of Bad Guy for sending him there? He knows he's eating up what remaining good years might lie ahead for me.

When I clean up the toilet floor and his rectum I find myself asking, "What did I do to deserve this duty?" I feel martyred and victimized. Often I don't even like him, mainly because of his self-absorption and non-communication. But who am I to complain of self-centeredness?

At times I feel compassionate and loving.

I judge myself as a not-nice human being, an unworthy wife (enter the Inner Patriarch), then become angry with having to live with such labels plastered on me (by myself, of course). What is, in fact, a decent person? I don't know. The answer depends on the judge, I still say. But any verdict I pass on myself is clearly self-serving.

I even somewhat exaggerate the ache in my back to excuse fully my attitude of "I shouldn't hoist him anymore; I can't."

I'm concerned, I admit, about my image with other people. Have I the guts to choose in behalf of my own best interests, accepting that one and all will think of me as they please?

I long for solitude. More and more, as I become increasingly aware of my emotions and honest about them, I appear to myself unfit—at least in my present stage—for marriage, intimacy, closeness. Damn it, I no longer want them. I vastly prefer the luxury of being who I am without any necessary concern for another's ego, rightful (?) claims, etc.

But I wish with all my heart that Adam's and my emotional connectedness hadn't ended in this fashion (monosyllabic and also confused on his part). I'll speak tritely and say "The world does seem to end not with a bang but a whimper."

(two weeks later)

Adam no longer can stand. I can't budge him

(two days later)

I choose the care facility where our internist heads the medical staff.

(one day later)

Our helper and I drive him to the nursing home. Adam comments, "Maybe here they can make me well." I feel quite touched by his hopefulness.

223

(five weeks later)

I learn from you, Adam, you've refused breakfast and lunch. You plan hereafter to forego all liquid, water included, and food. I warn you, "You'll be dead in a week." "That's the idea," you counter. "I've had it with this body."

I move into the nursing home to be near you. Not once does your determination to reject nourishment and liquid waver.

Your eyes regain for the first few days some vestige of their former twinkle. You laugh with attendants and our doctor. You've taken charge of yourself and again are in control of your life. Ill as you are, your air is one of empowerment. You talk little. I express my gratitude for our life together and my love of you. I regret that I didn't request some response, any.

Hospice workers come a few days before the conclusion of the two weeks you last. When your death arrives I'm holding your hand and stroking your forehead. Tranquilly you slip away.

Adam, I applaud and admire your courage in choosing death, your commitment to ending a life you now feel robbed of. Until you once more make it your own.

But I mourn your absence from this world.

27. JOURNALISMS: EIGHTEEN

(seventeen days later)

Adam, you've been dead six days. Is my experiencing no emotion about you or anything else retribution for my initial intolerance of your blocking feelings? Recalling my reactions I weep as I write.

(one day later)

I feel longing to embrace and hold, to be with, the man you were before your second fall.

(one day later)

To have you back I'd almost gladly accept the you of the last two and a half years. But to speak truth I wouldn't want you here at the price of continuing my lifestyle since your second fall. I'm referring to my nursing you, enduring the hired care here in the house, etc.

What I long for is the man before the episodes on the tennis court and in the kitchen—even preceding just your second hip disaster. But there's no going back to either time. Nor would I choose returning to life with the person you lately became.

The Adam I ache to put my arms around contracted Parkinson's, and to have you now I'd be stuck with the kind of existence I don't want. I well recall my inner cries to you and the world of the last, say, year: "Give me back my life." They were interspersed, of course, with other emotions, thoughts and wishes.

~ ~ ~ ~ ~ ~

I feel an obligation to give you, Adam, immortality by constant summoning of my memories of you. It seems my duty to you to remind myself of everything— and I do mean everything. Yet I realize that if I dig for recollections I'm not living in the present. I experienced our lives together at the time of their many happenings, which was the purpose of "the then," now fulfilled.

(one week later)

My theory as a medical amateur is this: Your first fracture resulted from the beginnings of a progressing Parkinson's disease. But at the time and until much later how was anyone to ascertain its possible occurrence?

(three months later)

A shift occurs, Adam, in my experiencing your death. I realize I've been reacting as if space contained its factness. Suddenly I grasp that there's no such factness other than in the heads of individuals. Your being dead now seems a white hole without boundary in the universe.

(one month later)

The difference is marked between being aware of your absence, Adam, missing you, and registering that you simply doesn't exist anymore, probably anywhere.

28. JOURNALISMS: NINETEEN

(eight months later)

I wish, Adam, I could claim a resolution of our basic conflict. I view it partly as my expressiveness colliding with your defensiveness. Or I perhaps could describe it as my assertiveness versus your assumption of innocence. I affirmed a right to speak out; you refuted perceived criticism invalidated for you by your policy of "don't make waves." Each of us struggled with the other to maintain our own autonomies.

In your last contribution to the subject, Adam, you did offer these admissions: For approximately a decade you'd branded me the culprit in our quarrels. You'd falsely considered the meanings of "I don't like it" and "You shouldn't have done it" to be identical. You'd assumed my reasons for talking were the same as yours but you now accepted their difference.

These statements of yours evidenced no particular emotion. I didn't feel they constituted a true breakthrough of insight. Prepared from past history for their reversal, I experienced no particular elation or sense of closure on our dilemma. And the issue lost its steam when your focus became your physical survival.

But we tried, Adam, we really did, to discover mutual ground for us to stand on. Perspectives change, so I suspect many seeming concurrences people claim prove temporary.

And I forgive us both the pain we caused each other.

(four months later)

I've new thoughts, Adam, about you and me.

In your view your stance of innocence rendered you inviolate. No one had a right to attempt reforming you. You never trusted me not to try.

But—hey!—how can I claim I'm not guilty of the attempt? Not when I struggled to persuade you that you should adopt my perspective on my articulations. I relinquished the attempt when I

227

chose to speak out only to honor my integrity. I believe you sensed my change. You no longer felt pressured to revise your view of me. Consequently, you could renounce your campaign to convert me to your assessment of my motivation.

Briefly put, we each conceded defeat in trying to change the other. We also retained our own identities.

I applaud the joys we shared. A large number of our days were consecutively not discordant but filled with mutual pleasure. We respected ourselves as basically decent persons. Our final truth is that we loved each other.

For me, at last our partnership feels complete

29. JOURNALISMS: TWENTY

(four months later)

Adam, I miss you more than ever. I confess I wouldn't want you back as you were your last several years. Not for me or you. But I wish intensely we could revert to an earlier time. My chief reason is:

My recent and particular confession rebounds. Yes, I tried to control you. How, mainly? By attempting to undercut your view of my motivation in speaking out. If I could relive our dialogue of that time, I'd assert myself differently. In what manner?

First, I'd request that you listen carefully. Again, as often before, I'd then explain my perspective. But these days I'd present it once only. I'd assure you I didn't intend to repeat my stand in the future. If you leveled charges at me similar to those of our past I'd respond briefly. Some possibilities: "You're entitled to your reaction but I don't agree with you." "The woman you're describing doesn't seem to fit me." "I hear you and I'm sorry you feel that way." Etc., etc.

When I began to speak out primarily for my own sake you already were conditioned to perceive me as coercive. I sympathize with you, Adam, in your dealings with me. I feel so cherishing of you that it pains me. I wish you were here, where I could put my arms around you and protect you from me.

I can't change who I was at that period of my life. I'm grateful to have grown into another vantage-point. I'm also engulfed by humbleness I don't quite understand.

A bit of light dawns. Even as I expressed myself mainly to honor my integrity, I judged you lacking. You failed, to my mind, in your not understanding the wisdom of my perspective on intimacy. I was still universalizing, considering it should be the norm for everyone. To me then, Adam, you were faulty in not embracing my arrogant, self-righteous message.

Now especially I've come more fully to realize that respecting individuality requires this: acceptance of all aspects of each person. I can dislike, yes, and speak my piece. But whether my message appeals is up to each person who hears it, and only to him or her. For therein lies the autonomy of each human being.

Adam, remembering us has taught me humility And more tenderness toward you and everyone. I love you perhaps more than ever before.

AFTERWORD

What prompted this postscript? Initially, my encounter with the cosmic generativity of love: its presence as tangibility. Ubiquitous in its forcefulness, it jarred my previous framings. These were articulated throughout this book so I shan't review them here.

My experience is scarcely unique. Many persons describe occurrences almost identical with mine. I suspect these visitations are often sustainable only briefly. For me, attentiveness to my present scene proves currently inducive.

How shall I connect my earlier beliefs with this newer happening? I hope by formulating the tenets that follow:

All is emptiness in self-manifestation as love.

Or:

Emptiness self-manifests entirely as love.

I'll more simply state:

The universe is love.

Perhaps I spare myself the sentimentality I dread by realizing this: The innumerable forms love adopts are totally individual and diverse.

Below I offer encapsulated suggestions I base on my five CONFESSIONS:

Philosophical: Explore

Spiritual: Subjectify

Meditational: Expand

Psychological: Allow

Marital: Accept. (This counsel is appropriate for all interpersonal relationships.)

Each one-word recommendation seems to me applicable to any of the book's sections.

All that is, including ourselves, are the mysteries and miracles of love.

Printed in the United States
29248LVS00002B/201

9 781413 755046